T0374454

Where Waters Meet

Beneath the Great Divide

CORAL BOUCHER

For book orders, email orders@traffordpublishing.com.sg

Most Trafford Singapore titles are also available at major online book retailers.

Printed in Singapore.

ISBN: 978-1-4907-0318-3 (sc)
ISBN: 978-1-4907-0319-0 (hc)
ISBN: 978-1-4907-0320-6 (e)

Library of Congress Control Number: 2013922878

Trafford rev. 01/23/2014

 www.traffordpublishing.com.sg

Singapore
toll-free: 800 101 2656 (Singapore)
Fax: 800 101 2656 (Singapore)

CONTENTS

SWIFTS CREEK

Swifts Creek Stream

I stood and breathed in the bush-scented air and the gentle zephyr whispered through my hair brushing my face lightly. The vista before me was a joy to behold, the blue—tinged hills surrounded the narrow valley and the golden blossom was like drops of gold from nature's brush. The varied colours of different trees chequered the landscape in a patchwork of colours.

That view was one to turn my brush repeatedly over the years, always seeking to bring it to life once again before my eyes. My frequent struggling efforts would fail, only to try again once more. My fingers surpassed by nature's brush.

That narrow valley was my home, loved always for its beauty and peace. It was there that I had spent my first twenty years. The three families living there then gave the place the name of 'Boucher Town'.

I was about twelve years old when I first climbed that hill, the smallest of those surrounding our home. Accompanied by my brother and cousins, I had set out, slowly but steadily, climbing the rough rocky and bushy hill. Making our way through Ti-Tree and scrub, scratches at face, arms and legs, we were delighted to see the myriad of coloured birds along our way. There were a great number of magpies, peewees, crows, and, high above us, a huge eagle, gliding and soaring and riding the air currents. He had his eye on the rabbits for his next meal. We stood in awe to see how he nabbed one. His incomparable eyesight enabled him to see from miles up in the sky the most luscious looking feast. When he had decided on the tastiest and plumpest one, he dropped like a stone at incredible speed, relying on his superb eyesight and great strength to nab his prey in his vicious talons. He then soared off into the sky to find a peaceful place to eat his meal. He was probably already thinking of some of the mice he had seen for the meal to come.

A kookaburra sat in a dead gum tree a few feet away— laughing at us, but he was also watching the eagle and, I'm sure, thinking that he would get there before him. The willy-wagtail sang his "sweet pretty creature" call to us, the magpie warbled and numerous other small birds joined in the orchestra of the bush. As we neared the peak, a small flock of sheep sheltering under the trees, took off, scampering away at our approach. We quickly dived in to take their places in the shade and sat appreciating the view before us and wishing we had brought a bottle of water with us.

Reaching the top, the vista opened before us with wattle trees in bloom and many other varieties of trees displaying their own particular shade of green, making a unique patchwork of colour on the surrounding hills. The birds' orchestra, the gentle, cooling breeze, along with the sparkling sunshine and enough clouds to make the sky interesting all added to the wonderful, perfect day nature had cloaked us in.

As we imbibed all this and wondered at it, our gazes fell to the hills across the way and to our left and right. Folding in they virtually enclosed the settlement in its own cosy little pocket which the stream had built as it had woven its way over the years along the valley floor.

We all agreed that it had been a wonderful day and we all appreciated our trek, which had taken us over four hours, and had been very strenuous. Ken remembers finding an eagle's nest among the trees at the top. I still remember it all fondly.

OUR GARDEN

We had a very large garden, with both flowers and vegetables and at least one of every type of fruit tree which could be grown in that area. I still miss the beautiful fruit and vegetables, freshly picked from trees and garden. There is no comparison with store bought fruit.

Mum, on her first visit back to Swift's Creek, after they had moved to Bairnsdale, was broken hearted to see that the person, who had bought the property, had bulldozed all the fruit trees and most of the flower garden. Why would anyone do that? It takes many years for a tree to bear fruit and would continue fruiting for many, many years with very little water or care required. Perhaps it was too difficult for him to eradicate some of the pests which would occur on some fruit trees. He may also have wanted to flatten the area to get rid of the mine workings on the property, but they were not close to the house where the flowers and orchard were.

Mum concentrated mainly on the flower garden and Dad, the vegetables. I loved gardening, and I was sure to be found out there in my spare time. It was the beginning of my great love of gardening which has brought immense joy and peace to me until this day. The very heavy frosts we experienced in our little valley made it a constant battle to keep some plants alive over winter and made it impossible to grow some varieties. At the risk of boring the non-flower lovers (if any) I'd like to mention all the different flowers, shrubs and trees Mum grew in our garden at "Emoh Rou".

I hope the joy of imagining the beautiful flowers for the flower lovers will outweigh any boredom and gritting of teeth of those

4

who will search franticly for the end of the list. In no particular order other than as I remember them, there were:-

The structured branches of the Japonica or Flowering Quince, which were a delight to arrange sparingly in a vase. There was the deep pink and the 'Apple Blossom' which was a very pale pink. The double flowering plum, both the white and pink, were an absolute delight with the double flowers all along the stem. The single May bush (Spirea) and the Spirea Anthony Waterer. It will take all day to extoll their individual virtues so I will just mention the names: The Chinese Beauty Bush and the Weigela, Camellias and Magnolias, Azaleas and Rhododendron, the Prunus, Buddleia and the Lilac. The flowering peach and the roses with most of their types and colours represented. The Mollis Azalea was a delight as it bloomed at different times to the Azalea. The Geraniums, Pelargoniums, the prickly native Gevillius, Hyacinths, Daffodils, Jonquils, Pinks and Carnations. The Chrysanthemums and the Dahlias, the Canna Lilies and Christmas lilies, the Primulas and Primroses and Grape Hyacinth, Hellabours, Gladioli and Asters, Russell Lupins and Larkspur and Delphinium, Daisies, Heuchera, Stocks and Pansies. The Violas and Anemones and Ranunculus, Wisteria and Weeping Cherry.

In this long list I'm sure I have missed some of those which grew and thrived in our garden. If you think of one I'm sure it was there. Mum always said that as much as the garden gave her very great delight, it doubled in the thought of it giving delight to others. All her gardens wherever she was, and mine, were built on this premise.

Mum and Dad's Wedding

TREES

A tree not seen very often now is the Kurrajong tree. They were a shapely tree with pretty but small and insignificant flowers. The seed capsule was unique, being a boat shape when split open with very hairy seeds aligned like rowers along the middle. The seed pods were prized for flower arranging. There was at least one of each fruit tree which all bore fruit in their seasons. Some of the apple trees had other varieties grafted on. One apple tree not in our garden, but up near the wattle daub cottage was the snow apple. It was a very old tree and probably heritage listed. Its skin was bright red, but the flesh wash snow white and a very sweet and distinctive taste.

Other old apple trees in that orchard may have been heritage. There was a good strong row of gooseberries, the true Gooseberries (not Chinese). They are seen occasionally now in the supermarket, but very expensive. The bushes were very prickly and very hardy as I don't recall them ever having water put on them. The fruit was a tasty berry, not too sweet but preserved in syrup were a luxury. Several large walnut trees were on that piece of land and a very large bed of asparagus.

Other trees on our property, but not in our garden, were the quince, the fruit of which is very hard but beautiful when stewed with cream on them. Another unusual use of the quince, other than bottling them was to roast them with the potatoes and pumpkin. A very tasty and piquant addition to the roast meal. The fig trees were a much loved fruit when they were able to be saved from the birds. It was common to see an old dress of Mums up in a tree as a scarecrow.

WATER RACE

Another challenge in keeping our verdant crops alive in the early days was water. To this end, Dad and my uncle reopened and maintained the water race which was originally built for goldmine workings, the diggings and mines from which still remained on our property. The creek at our place was quite a long way from the house and any relatively level ground, and too far away and too steep to cart any large quantity of water. This race was a narrow man-made canal, roughly two to three feet wide and about two feet deep, dug into the side of the cliff and following the line of the river. It began many miles upstream rising from a dam built in the creek and relied on gravity to allow the water to flow. Those old time gold-miners, perhaps Chinamen, must have been very clever to get the fall right to make the water flow by gravity. It took quite a lot of effort to keep it running. There were no concrete or metal pipes for the water to flow through so the banks of the race would break away and we would have no water.

It was all hands on deck to fix it and I can remember standing knee deep in the often freezing water, trying to build the wall again with rocks, sticks, logs and whatever we could find to make it strong again. We hoped that the kangaroos, wallabies and wombats didn't get digging in there again too quickly. When the water at last reached our property, it was run along shallow ditches between the rows of vegetables and again, was gravity fed to water our garden. The race, after doing its job in watering our gardens, continued on its way to my uncle's house next door and after completing its chores there, crossed a wide pit, also made by gold-miners, through a flume. The flume, from my memory, was made with thick bark, wrapped around with wire to form a pipe. It may have been a hollow log, but I am at a loss to know how this would have been achieved. Once having navigated its way through the flume, the race continued along the back of the property and at last, joined the creek as it followed a wide bend past our properties. This was our main source of water in those days, but water tanks were later put up to provide water for the house.

THE VALLEY—THE EELS

Another benefit of the race was the eels which came down until the netting fence was met. We would scoop the eels up squealing and shrieking as the slippery long slithering fish tried to escape us, wrapping around our arms and often sliding away from us. They took some time to catch and then we would take them home for our meals. Luckily we all enjoyed the taste whether smoked, done in egg and bread-crumbs, or in batter. Eels and rabbits, along with the bounteous lovely fresh offerings from our garden, formed a very large part of our diet at that time and for many years to come.

Another popular dish at our table which was very good for eking out our meagre resources was 'Mock Fish'. This delicacy was made by stripping the green leaves off the stalks of spinach or silver beet. The stalks were cut into roughly five or six long pieces and dipped in batter. These battered strips were then fried in dripping until golden brown. We all loved this dish and there was always plenty for seconds because we always had a beautiful big stand of silver beet, richly green, crinkly and healthy. The leaves were not wasted, as they were shredded and boiled and coated with spicy butter to add greens to the menu with our 'fish'.

CYANIDE

A major question raises its head now, which was apparently not thought of at the time and even until this day, remains.

Just half to one mile from the dam, from which the water was diverted to the race, was a very large heap of mine tailings.

These tailings were what were left after the crushed rock was separated from the gold. This whole area was a huge gold-mining place. Cyanide, a very dangerous poison, was used in this smelting process and all the children and of course adults were warned to keep away from this site.

When it rained the soil and gravel was washed down the hill and entered the Riley's Creek which flowed into Swift's Creek from which our race was drawn. The query to this day is whether enough cyanide remained in the water when it reached us to cause any problems and whether it was the cause of the myriad health problems in our family.

CASSILLIS

Only a short way beyond the tailings heap was a very large mine, tunnelled into the side of the hill, that one and another were sufficiently safe to go a short way into. The King Cassillis mine was re-opened not too long ago and was again put into production. These mines were not far from the small township of Cassillis.

Cassillis was a very large, thriving township during the gold-mining days and the hotel and school-room still stood and were occupied in my younger days. The cemetery still remains and was a venue for 'back-to' celebrations recently.

I remember going with Dad when he delivered vegetables and fruit. I would sit in the 'dickey-seat' of the old A or T-model Ford. The dickey-seat was put in the place similar to the boot of more modern cars, but would open and be pulled down rather than lifting it up. It was not very comfortable, but I enjoyed any trip with my beloved Dad.

One memory that sticks in my mind was of a huge metal or clay bowl which one lady would bring out to have filled with vegetables. It was not like the old tin bath we would bathe in each week but much flatter. I am yet to see it's like again.

WHEN THE COWS
COME HOME

The hill at the front of the house, as mentioned before, was the paddock in which the cows which needed to be milked spent their days. It was one of my daily tasks to bring them home each night. I would set off, by going left, hoping they had not gone right, and vice-versa. I would be calling to the cows all the time, hoping that they would hear me and come towards home before I had walked all the way to the end of the paddock in that direction. As night was drawing near, the further I went through Ti-tree scrub and rocky and steep ground, I was invariably in tears before I found them. To the right were several disused mine shafts and this was not my favourite direction at that time of day. Although the trees had been cleared more in that direction, a lot of suckers still remained. Suckers were young shoots which had grown up after the trees had been ring-barked. To explain, ring-barking was cutting through the bark with an axe all the way around the tree which stops the sap from rising and eventually kills the tree. Trees needed to be killed and cleared away to make more space for feed to grow for the animals. New shoots usually shot out below the cuts and had to be knocked off with a mattock. We children would be included in carrying out this job. It was a seemingly long and tedious chore compared with the current method of tree-felling, but was one approach used in those days, without the help of any other labour-saving-devices to clear the ground for farming.

Once home the cows needed to be milked. At that time we were milking about four cows morning and night. Luckily they spent the night in a smaller, closer paddock. One cow, 'Trixie' (all the cows had names) was a real rogue. She would jump all the fences and get away. Dad eventually put a device on her which stopped her errant ways: The device was two long sticks tied to her neck on each side. These were long enough, so that when Trixie tried to jump the fences, no matter how high she jumped, they would catch on the top of the fence and stop her in her tracks.

MORE CHORES

Another evening chore I would do was to collect morning sticks. We had wood stoves and fires and they were much easier to light with smaller sticks and bark which was also called kindling.

As I had other jobs to do, I was often late getting to this one and night would be closing in.

As I was a 'fraidy-cat', I would jump at every shadow and thought that behind every dark tree was potentially a 'boogie man' waiting to get me. I was, as usual, in tears before getting home.

I was often very jealous of the other girls who lived in town and didn't have to do such onerous chores. But as the eldest child, my next brother being five years younger than me, and Mum and Dad busy with their own chores, it fell to me. I guess it made me tougher to face the future.

THE SCRUBBINGS

Clothes Boiling Copper

The earliest experience I remember, in regard to clothes washing, was when the water had to be heated in a kerosene tin on a fire outside. We scrubbed the clothes on an old wash-board and then put the water and clothes in the kerosene tin to boil. The wash board was a rectangular piece of wood in some cases, in others, some sort of metal. The timber had ripples in it. Scrubbing the clothes against the ripples would help to clean them. Different materials like tin and galvanised iron were used to make the rippled area. The earliest method of soaping the clothes I recall was using a big, long cake of 'Velvet Soap'. This was cut into smaller squares and scrubbed onto the clothes on the washboard. Later an old knife was used to scrape shavings of soap into the kerosene tin to boil up the clothes with it.

A later invention was a wire cage with long handles. The handles and cage opened up to enable us to put a square of soap in. With the cage closed and catch fixed, the gadget was then 'swished' through the water to add soap without burning oneself in the boiling water.

Another small, but much used invention, was the 'Blue Bag'. This little bag contained a knob of blue. After some research I found that it was made from synthetic ultra-marine and baking soda. Used in colonial times and still available today, this was a wonderful little bag of tricks. Swirled around in the rinsing water until the water is sky blue, your whites, when dried on the line, will come out a dazzling white. Much safer than the bleach used today. Another excellent use is for soothing bites and stings. Even today it is sworn by amongst grandmothers and mums. It was particularly good for bee stings and ant bites.

In recent times, these old washboards were hunted up for 'skiffle bands'. The musician would rub his fingers or spoons, or sticks, over the ripples to make music. The skiffle band also used tea chests with a hole drilled in it. A piece of cord was taken through this hole and up to be tied to the top of a stick attached to the chest. Music was made by plucking the cord with the fingers and manipulating the stick back and forth to produce different notes. The tea chests were also used as drums.

ON THE LINE

Once the clothes had boiled enough, they would be fished out (after much poking and prodding with a stick which was furry and pale from the constant dunking in hot water).

The clothes were then put into clean water to rinse. Cold water I'm pleased to say, as we then wrung them out by hand. Mum was always very good at wringing out as her hands had become very strong and this was very hard on the hands.

STARCH

The tablecloths, hankies, dresses, pillow-slips and aprons, were put through a light starch rinse. This final rinse was to ensure those particular things would have a slightly stiffened finish when ironed. The pleats in pinnies (as aprons were called), dresses and such things would retain their shape.

After being wrung-out they would be pegged, still dripping, onto a rope which was strung between two poles. The line was then held up higher in the air by a 'prop', often just a forked stick. This prop enabled the clothes to be kept off the ground and to be lifted up higher to catch the breeze. This breeze, or even wind, was always wished for on Mondays. The washing day. Not wished for was a very strong wind which would have our washing ending up in the bush.

A later use for starch was Mum and I used to crochet and knit many things. Clothes and jumpers were knitted and other special things were crocheted. One thing we loved to do in my teenage years was to crochet white swans. The pattern for these has long gone. Maybe someone still has a pattern? There was the swan and something else. Maybe a large waterlily?

We would crochet the swans and put them through a very thick starch. When they were almost dry, all starched articles needed to be sprinkled with water and then rolled together to make them just damp. This made them much easier and better to iron. We would carefully iron the swans into shape and they would sit up beautifully.

We would put them on stalls for church, mothers' club and the many others we worked for. They would go quite well just as they were as an ornament or we filled them with home-made sweets or some such specialties.

Dolly pegs were also used then which were carved out of a soft wood and often had a further career as little girls' dolls. Dollied up with a scrap of rag, string hair and a dash of paint for the facial features, they were treasured by little girls who had little else to play with.

Best Time Of The Week

We carted hot water from the kerosene drum, and later from the copper, for our weekly baths. The water was topped up with hot water for each person starting with Mum and ending with Dad. We all scrubbed and scrubbed as quickly as we could because someone was always yelling at us to "Hurry up! You're taking too long!" I know I always loved bath night.

I felt, and probably smelled, so much fresher and cleaner with clean undies and pyjamas and clean clothes to start the school week. This weekly bathing would be something very hard to imagine now by children with their daily ablutions in this day and age.

We later progressed to a chip-heater which was a large, tall cylinder into which the water was poured and under that was an area into which the chips were piled and set alight. It would make a queer 'chuffing noise' and when the tap was turned on, and the water hot enough, it would hiss and splutter

WOOD-WORK

Because all our cooking and heating was done on wood fires and stoves, we used a lot of wood. Fortunately we had a lot of dead trees on another part of the farm.

It would be a combined effort with Mum and Dad. We kids and my uncle and aunt and our cousins would also all be involved, armed with the necessary tools for the task and lunch and cold water, or tea, for us all.

We would all head to this area, sometimes a not so easy task as, above the paddock where we must go, was very often quite wet and slippery. I, of course, would be squealing as we slipped and slid. I imagined us all down the bottom of the hill with the saw bench on top of us.

Perhaps a small spring was rising somewhere above there, keeping the ground constantly moist, and with the help from any recent rain, that particular place was impassable. Our expedition would then have to be called off. Luckily we had another place to get wood from but it was not so good.

The process was then begun. If the trees were already felled, we would trim off the branches and would roll the logs down from higher up the hill to a relatively flat area. Thump! Crash! they went, sometimes quickly and straight, and others more slowly, stopping part way down. "Shift it!" came the cry and someone would dash out and straighten it up. Sometimes there would come a cry "It's stuck!" and a couple of others would rush in to help.

If we were lucky we would get most of them trundling obediently down the hill with someone there to stop them at the right level above the trailer.

On another day, well, they would nearly all get caught on a rock. Or maybe the branches had not been trimmed close enough to the trunk and these ones would, by Murphy's Law, almost always get caught up and it would be a battle getting it down.

The air was turning blue and sweat would be pouring off our faces but we turned once more to the task. About three logs went down fairly well.

"OK" said Dad, "We're cooking with gas now. Just a couple more, then smoko." "Right!" we yelled and stuck back in, sending them down quickly.

Then, there was this big one. It took more than one of us to get it started.

"Good one" we'd say and started it off. It started slowly then, sped up, gaining speed with every turn. Then it hit a rock, sending it off track, and, still going at great speed, hit another which sent it flying into the air. "Look out!" came the cry and everyone, including the dogs, scuttled for cover. There wasn't much cover down there, so they all raced, helter-skelter, some one side and some the other. We stood up there not knowing what to do. That log could go anywhere! Then, with a mighty crunch, it hit a bigger rock and smash! "Look out! Help! Mummy!" Gosh. Heck. Golly. It exploded! Hundreds of pieces flew everywhere! Wow! "Yip yip yip" said the dog, as it raced off with its tail between its legs. That big thick, tough, scary log was hollow inside. The smaller pieces landing on the trailer, car, dog, and saw-bench with just the dust and rotted out wood landing on everyone in reach. "Well that's one we won't have to split" said one wit. We all agreed that we deserved a drink of tea and a sandwich, albeit with a few 'extras' in some cups with much spitting and squirting.

At one stage we had a horse which would, by having a chain attached to his harness and this hooked around the log, be able to snig the logs down to the saw-bench. The saw-bench was attached to a back wheel of the old Dodge. I thought they would have taken the tyre off but Ken said he remembers a large belt being twisted into a figure of eight, and two crow bars being driven into the ground to hold the belt taut. One of the older children was pressed into controlling the speed of the saw from the front of the car.

We would be at the hand throttle and from behind would come the shouts "Right, get going slowly. No! Not so fast," or "Faster, slow down" or "STOP!" or some other derogatory remarks.

We enjoyed this part of the job as we thought we were being very useful and had control in our hands. We felt very proud of ourselves. The adults and older kids, not otherwise engaged, would be at the back. One or two would be picking up the logs and passing them to the sawyer, who would push the wood through the saw, to have it cut in lengths for each individual stove. Another would be pulling the cut pieces away and still another would be stacking them into the trailers. This trailer stacking job had to be done properly and every log stacked neatly as it was necessary to take as much as possible in each load. Once the trailer loads were home, we all would unload them on to each wood-heap.

We would also take home the stumps of trees to be used as a 'backlog' in the open fireplaces. A 'backlog' was the word for a large piece of wood, as big as would fit in, often the stump of the tree with the roots still attached. This was placed at the back of the big open fireplaces. Once the smaller wood was burnt, this backlog would do its job by burning away for a long time. Often quite late into the night.

A cosy night in front of that big open fire, with the sparks flying and the snap and crackle and glow of different colours of the different gases burning, the heat turning our faces and legs red, the family all grouped around perhaps roasting walnuts and perhaps a sing-along. Ah! The memory comes back to me of those wonderful winter nights long gone when we were all together and happy.

However, I tarry.

Some wood might be split as soon as it reached the individual wood heaps, if badly needed then. However, usually the wood be split later as needed, often by the women and I can remember chopping my leg with the axe even as a relatively young girl. Those not involved in the wood getting at any time were sent off to another job.

NOXIOUS WEEDS

Ken can remember hoeing 'blanket-weed'. Sounds a bit like those cosy winters—but far from it. This was a weed with long leaves feeling and looking like pieces of grey blanket in a rosette shape just above the ground. If left to grow it would produce a tall spike with pretty yellow flowers. These pretty yellow flowers would self-seed prolifically and produce many more. This was declared a noxious weed by the Lands Department and a farmer could be fined if he had not made an attempt to eradicate this from his farm. It could be hoed out fairly easily with a mattock but it was almost always growing in rocky soil which made the job harder.

Blanket-weed and thistles, 'Patterson's Curse' and blackberries were the bane of a farmer's life. Many other times when not getting wood we would be out hoeing them out. The hoe was a very handy tool and the long handled sickle was a great tool for the blackberries.

The Most Exciting Day

Eventually came the most exciting day when, after building an extension for our new bathroom, Dad installed pipes and taps for the hot and cold water.

What a marvel!

PIONEER MOTHER

When my mother first went to Swift's Creek she had to wash clothes in the creek and the cooking for the family she looked after was done on a fire outside. She gathered and chopped the wood for her outside fire and cooked on this fire outside. She often told me she made bread in a Dutch-Oven. Perhaps it would be more like Damper.

The light at night was produced by candles. There were none of the conveniences we have today. We even go camping for a weekend or longer with more mod-cons than they had in those days! They washed outside in a big dish until the luxury of a tin bath came along.

Mum would make aprons and sometimes girls' dresses and pinnies with flour bags. Even hessian sacks were utilised in this way. Some were used for bedding and also the actual bed. The bed was made with long branches and the hessian sacks swung between those branches. Hessian was also nailed up to make 'walls' in the huts.

I regret that I did not glean more information from her during these tough times.

Hessian sacks were used for many different things, those aforementioned and also for covering tender plants to keep off the very heavy frosts. They were also used for mats to wipe our shoes, to drape over shoulders to keep off a shower of rain and even to carry things. I think Dad used to take his lunch in a sack to work at one time. Some were even used to carry rabbits home. There was one time when I took the rabbit's home alive in the sacks. I had caught them in the traps and was not strong enough in the wrists to be able to wring their necks.

Mum came to Swift's Creek after her marriage to Dad, on the back of his motorbike. Can you imagine the trip from Geelong in those days and not on a modern motor bike with all its modern improvements either?

On research I found an article which said, quote, 'It was hard to find a more remote place in Victoria than Swift's Creek,' unquote.

Those winding roads must have been in so much worse condition than I remember. The very steep hills and sharp corners and the long, long way between stops. The corrugations would almost shake you off the road when going round a corner.

The coaching stops and places to change horses and bullocks were quite a fair way apart. The different names still signed on this road, would often be a place to stop in those days. It would, in those days take more than one day to travel between Swift's Creek and Bairnsdale, our nearest large town.

OFF TO THE 'BIG SMOKE'

The first trip to my Grandmother's home in Geelong that I can recall was a cause of real excitement. We would go almost every Christmas to see Mum's family, but the first trip I can recall was when I was a young child.

The biggest magical thrill was when we pulled a cord hanging from the ceiling and guess what! A light came on! Wow!

This was obviously before we had electricity and all the wondrous work and time-saving appliances and gadgets which came with this.

THE LITTLEST ROOM

We still had to go around the back of the big sandstone mansion to the toilet in a little hut. Here, you sat over a bowl with water in it and when finished, you pulled a chain and more water rushed down into the bowl from a container above and cleaned it. It was all magical.

On returning home, things were still very different. We went to our outside toilet in a hut around the back of the house. But what was different was the hut was built over a deep hole.

This was called a 'long drop'. Inside, there was a wooden board across the drop, at a height for you to sit on. This board had a hole into which you placed your bottom. I was always afraid the hole was too big and I could fall through. It didn't smell very nice and Mum would tip Phenyl down it and Dad often threw lime and soil down to cover the contents.

We cut up paper into squares, threaded a piece of wire through and hung this on a nail and used this for toilet paper. Not nearly so soft as today's offering. It was too bad if you became interested in an article as the rest of it was invariably gone.

Another scary thing was the spiders. We would often see them in there and we had all been warned about Red-Backs. Being such a scaredy-cat and with a good imagination, I thought that they could be under the seat and bite me on the bottom. Another result of my imagination was that I thought I had seen a snake down in the hole and that the inevitable could happen. None of these nasties did occur but I would be off and away from there as soon as possible! Even when I was a teenager I would not go down there at night. I would have the necessary under the bed.

Still on that subject, at school in my first few years, there was a different style of toilet. Mostly everything was the same as the long-drop, but instead of the hole underneath it, there was a flap at the back through which the boys on duty took and replaced the large filled cans. They then took them away to a hole which had been dug a longer distance away from the schoolrooms.

COOLGARDIE SAFE

To keep our butter and milk and all our perishables cool, we had a Coolgardie safe which was a cupboard with wet hessian bags hanging down on all sides into a pan at the bottom into which the water drained. The water, as the hessian dried, was drawn up by osmosis to the top again. Yet another use for hessian sacks.

I recall someone at that time, probably in town or Geelong, had a more 'up-to-date' model. It was an icebox, more like our modern fridges to look at, but had a compartment to accommodate a big block of ice. The iceman came each day to replace the melted ice block. He carried the ice with a device for carrying it which was a handle at the top and prongs each side which dug in and gripped the ice.

The next refrigerator was the one run by kerosene as you would imagine. Trimming the wick and keeping the fuel topped up was all the attention it required.

Then came the 32 volt fridge as this became available, which was a lot kinder on our noses. The kerosene being burnt in the previous model was very smelly.

CANDLES TO LAMPS

Lighting at night progressed from candles to lanterns, which were lamps which could be carried by the handle, around outside. These were run by filling the tank with kerosene. They had a wick which soaked up the kerosene, which was burnt to provide the flame to see by.

There was a handy little gadget attached to the frame, which held the glass and with which you could lift it up to light the wick.

One had to be careful not to have the wick too high as this resulted in the flame flaring up and blackening the glass. This would have to be cleaned at once, as the lantern shed no light at all with a black glass. We had more than one in the house, but it was necessary to carry one with you to another room and to take outside to light our way.

An improvement on the lantern, and a better light for inside, were, in those days before electricity, 'Aladdin' lamps. These were tall lamps with a bowl to hold the kerosene, and a wick which soaked up the fuel. This wick was lit and provided the light, the brightness of which could be achieved by turning a knob at the side to raise or lower the wick. The whole thing was then topped with a tall glass which would protect the flame.

Another clever invention was the wall light. It was filled with kerosene, as were the lamps and had the wick and glass but had a tin plate which protected the wall from the flame and had a hook from which you could hang it. A regular chore was to clean all the lamp glasses as these would become black from the flame, especially when the wick was turned up too high.

An even better lamp later became available which was the Tilley Lamp. The fuel and glass was the same principle but, instead of the wick, a mantle was lit. This was a little net bag, made from some sort of fine cloth with drawstrings at top and bottom. This mantle was attached to the top of the pipe, which came from the fuel bowl, by the drawstrings. The mantle was lit and had to be 'burnt in.'

This was achieved by maintaining a steady, low light which must completely cover the mantle. Once this was achieved, the mantle became a fragile web of ash hanging together. Great care had to be taken to not touch this or to shake the lamp too much. The result of this carelessness would be that the mantle would crumble and fall down. Just a useless piece of ash. Even touching it with the match when lighting it would mean disaster. As the mantles, bought in packets of two at the store, were not cheap, everyone was warned of dire consequences should a mantle be wasted. The lamp was then pumped up with a small pumping device in the fuel bowl. The greater the pressure, the brighter the light.

THE FLAT IRON

Another necessity in those days, which operated under the same principal, was the kerosene-fuelled iron for ironing clothes. The fuel tank would be pumped up and the more pressure, the more heat. Previous models of irons were the Flat Iron with handle attached, which was heated on the stove. A thick rag was needed as the handle became as hot as the iron's bottom. We would have several of these at a time on the stove. As the heat was used from one, another hot one was chosen. A bit of spit on the finger, a very quick touch to the iron, and a listen for the hiss, was the very scientific and best method to ensure if it was hot enough for the job.

The fire needed to be stoked up and throwing out a lot of heat for this important job.

The next model was the more oval-shaped iron, more like a boat shape and lighter and easier to use. It came complete with a detachable handle which clicked into the top of the hot iron. This breakthrough ensured that the handle didn't get too hot, as it was not attached to the iron whilst it was heating.

Whatever the model, another piece of rag was needed to wipe the bottom of the iron to remove any black created from the stove.

Then along came the petrol or kerosene model as previously described.

We usually had a salt-sprinkled rag to wipe the bottom of the iron to clean it before placing it on the clothes to be ironed. I usually ironed all my clothes, taking care with a damp pressing cloth to press the pleats into my winter school tunic. Each week this job was done with a sponging of any spots off with a vinegar-soaked rag.

My blazer got the same treatment but without the pesky pleats. My Brownie and Guide uniforms needed to be pressed very carefully with the scarf sprinkled with water, along with other starched things such as hankies and pillow-slips, rolled all in together to make them just damp and easier to get all the wrinkles out. I took great care of all my uniforms as I took pride in them.

THE HUMBLE STOVE

These early stoves were black iron stoves with a firebox on top in which the wood was burnt. A very ingenious invention. The top had several holes with lids. The lids could be lifted to get a pot heating more quickly. The Damper in the flue was used to control the amount of air the fire would have. The whole top lifted off to enable toast to be made on a long, extendable fork, or to heat the room. The firebox was cleaned of ash and charcoals each morning to be set ready to light the fire for the day.

If more heat was required in the oven, a lot of wood and some kindling was added to get it roaring, sometimes catching fire to the inside of the chimney.

Often a cry would go up "The oven's hot! What about making some scones?" Or, if we had run out of bread, we would make a scone loaf, which was one large scone. More like a damper. We would then have bread for our lunches. It was quite an art to achieve the correct temperature for each item to be cooked. With no temperature gauge, the heat was judged by the experienced cook, by checking the temperature of the oven's handle.

In the very cold mornings we would all gather around the stove as it was the only heating in the house at that hour. You would be very lucky if you could get the right spot to warm your feet near the opened oven. This stove must be stoked at all times and not allowed to go out during the day unless it was summer and too hot.

Then Mum may decide to have a meal for which the stove would not be needed. Perhaps a salad or 'bread and scrape-it' This meal was not infrequently used, depending on what was at hand. Scrape-it being jam, home-made, or cheese or Vegemite or in the leaner days, dripping. I quite enjoyed the toast and dripping, especially if I was lucky enough to get a bit of meat juice with it.

The stove was also used at one stage to heat a big rectangular urn which sat permanently on the top and to the side with a tap to draw the water from.

At one stage we had a really huge black cast iron kettle which also had the tap in front. This became a very popular antique over the years, often used for putting plants into.

This hot water was used for baths, dishes, cleaning etc. until we progressed to another model. The old black stove was a marvellous thing and did a wonderful job for us all at that particular time. The open fire in the lounge was lit later on but usually only at night or weekends when we were all at home.

One drawback was cleaning and polishing it with stove black and old rags. We would use plenty of elbow grease to make it gleam.

A later model of stove was the slow combustion stove. This wondrous invention was able to be stoked and shut right down at night. In the morning, it would only need a poke with the poker and some smaller sticks and away it would go.

Another very handy gadget was a thermometer in the oven door. With this we were able to reach the correct temperature by adding some more wood and opening it up for more heat or closing it down to decrease the temperature. As with the old black stove, we became more adept at reaching the correct temperature for each item we intended to bake. There was still the odd cry of "The oven's hot! How about some scones!" but this was mainly said in jest, as everyone knew that neither Mum nor I would have the very few minutes it took to whip up a batch.

HOT WATER ON TAP

Another improvement was that the water was piped into a large holding and heating tank at the back of the stove. Consequently, hot water was then piped to the taps at the kitchen sink and the bathroom. In the summertime it was not essential to have the stove going all the time, as the water in the holding tank would remain hot enough for a couple of days.

I'm not sure how Dad managed with his cuppa with this new stove when it was allowed to go out. Dad would swig from his cup, poured out of the teapot in which someone had made a cup of tea earlier, whenever he was in the house. The tea would often stew for hours and become like tar. He would continue to swig away at it black and no matter how strong and hot it was if the stove was hot. He would also drink it cold so I guess the new stove did not upset his habit too much. He did not pass up a fresh cuppa though when it was brewed and would then continue as before. When vacuum flasks were invented, his water would be kept hot for his tea.

WHITEWASH

The open wood fireplaces would be painted with whitewash. This was made by mixing some white powder with water. The thicker the liquid, the better coverage you would get. We would make sure the fire was out, clean all the charcoal and ashes and gave it a good sweep down. We would then paint the inside of the fireplace and as far as we could reach up the chimney. This treatment would make the fireplace look clean and bright. But, because of the nature of its use, it didn't stay nice for long. I think the stove and fireplace were done each week.

This white-wash powder could be bought at the local store, but we were lucky to have some pipe clay up in a gully. This pure-white pipe clay was consequently much sought after by potters. I don't believe there was a great deal of it. It had been discovered when rabbits had scratched some out whilst digging to make their burrow.

This white-wash was also used as a cheap way to brighten up walls, sheds and fences. Even the chook pen was painted.

BAKING

Mum was an excellent cook and her sponges, scones, chocolate cakes, biscuits and slices were greatly appreciated by all.

In those days, if someone came for afternoon tea, supper or whatever, the table was usually spread with at least three different slices, cakes and biscuits or whatever baking was to hand. There was almost always a dry biscuit or dainty sandwich with tomato with cheese and ham as well to suit all tastes.

This was the norm in whatever home you visited in those days. The table was usually spread with a lace or other pretty tablecloth, nice cup, saucer and plates and a desert fork to enable you to negotiate these often cream-filled delicacies.

Just as well Mum and I loved to cook.

I would often spend all day or even two at the weekend cooking cakes, slices, batches of biscuits, one after another. Dad's favourite was a coconut raspberry slice so I always made sure there were some there for him. We made Lamingtons, sponges, ginger-fluff, fruit cake, Yo-Yo biscuits and Anzacs. Also cream-puffs along with a chocolate slice which was a biscuit base covered with marshmallow and topped with a layer of melted chocolate. Many more delicacies were produced, depending on what we felt like cooking at the time.

Mum would often be washing up behind me as I baked away to my heart's content. Strangely, everyone ate like that in those days and no-one was obese.

Needless to say that this was not the case during the depression but at this time, food and money were not so scarce.

COPING WITH THE CROP

Along with drying our apricots and apples, another way we saved our fruit and vegetables was by bottling them. Almost all our fruit was bottled successfully. Apricots, peaches, pears, apples, plums, cherries, nectarines and even grapes.

This bottling was done as follows. The fruit was washed and cut into appropriate shapes and placed in preserving jars. These were special jars with a wider neck and made from Pyrex-type glass which was heat-resistant.

Once the correct number of jars for a batch was filled, syrup of water mixed with sugar was poured into the top of each jar. A special thick rubber band seal was then placed on, followed by the lids. The lids were then fastened on with clips, especially made to seal the jars. The jars were then placed into a large tin vat. Water was then added to fill the container half way up the sides of the bottles.

Placing the vat on the stove and adding a special thermometer to a niche in the side of the container, we added a lid. The whole lot was then set to boil the water to the correct temperature for the particular variety of fruit. A book was provided with the bottling kit, to detail the correct temperature. It was essential to reach the correct temperature to vacuum-seal the lids to the bottles. Once the correct temperature was reached, the water was allowed to cool and the bottles taken out of the bath. The jars must be allowed to completely cool before the clips were taken off. If the lids were not sealed on correctly then the whole process would have to be repeated. If the lids did not seal properly, then the contents would have to be thrown away as it was dangerous to keep the contents. If it had only been for a couple of days, it would be safe to stew up the fruit which could then be eaten quickly within a day or so.

Vegetables, in particular, had to be dealt with as instructed. Botulism poisoning was and still is a very real danger.

However, knowing of the danger, and taking care, this Fowler's method of bottling fruit is a very easy and safe way to make sure your fruit is not wasted. This system is still available today but with a more sophisticated model for those who are prepared to take the trouble. Even an electric model came into play. I had my eye on one for a long time but could never justify the expense.

It was scandalous for Mum in these more recent times to see fruit trees laden with fruit and just falling to the ground for the want of picking.

Did these people not know what a valuable asset they had to hand and that fruit tasted so much better than that bought from the shop? There is no comparison. I still mourn for the taste of fruit (and vegetables) freshly picked from the tree or garden. Mum, even in her late eighties, having a few fruit trees in her back yard, could not bear to see the fruit wasted. She would give a lot away to family and friends, and take them to her beloved Seniors Club.

She would have rags and even a complete dress (acting as a scarecrow) to try to discourage the birds and lamented the fact that the birds were pecking the fruit when it was not yet ripe. Once the fruit was ripe, she was out there picking it.

She continued with stewing and freezing in containers, still having some in the freezer from past years. She would make jam, mainly to give away or to put on stalls as, being a diabetic, was unable to eat much herself.

The fruit was always easy to use in the times when it was out of season. We could open a bottle of fruit, add a pot of custard or ice cream or cream and a delicious sweet was immediately to hand, even for unexpected guests. We also made jam from all the different varieties of fruits including apple, grape and quince jelly made from the skins and cores of the fruit only.

Apricot jam was one of the most popular, but blackberry jam was also one of the favourites. Nectarine, peach, plum, and loganberry were more of them. We would be very busy in the fruit season, squirrelling away our reserves for the next year.

We always made enough to see us through till the next season. There was also plenty to put onto stalls at fetes or street stalls and to give to others who did not have the necessary fruit, time, or inclination to make their own.

Tomato and plum sauce was also added to our now bulging larder. All winter we would have stewed tomatoes from our bottled store. We all liked tomato cooked with onion, on toast.

We would often have it for breakfast, or with chops and mashed potatoes. We would have bottled tomato added to pasta and minced beef.

If chops were on the menu, the cry, originating from Dad, would be "Chops for tea, wash your hands!" This was jokingly said, as we at no time came to the table without washing our hands.

We did always pick up the bones in our hands as we considered the best meat, closest to the bone, would be wasted.

Vacuum tub for Preserving fruit

Nailed

Dad was always building something, adding on to our timber cottage which he had built himself. There would be new cupboards and extensions and outdoors he would add tank stands, garden edges and new paths. One extension, which was to be our new bigger kitchen and bathroom, was the scene of an unexpected drama.

I was climbing over the floor joists towards Dad. Unbeknown to me, my baby brother, who was only eighteen months old and not too steady on his feet, was following me.

I heard an unusual noise, and, whipping around I saw Ken, screaming his lungs out with a piece of board *stuck to his head*! Upon looking further we found, much to our surprise and horror, that the board was attached to his head by a two inch nail.

Mum, on hearing the kerfuffle, dashed out, and with great foresight, plucked Ken up and dashed with him to the car with Dad right behind her. Dad drove off at a great pace with Ken cradled carefully in Mum's arms. We were left standing and wondering how Ken was and how badly he was hurt.

It was a long wait till they came home, but fortunately the bush nurse had been at her clinic in town, about three miles away, and was able to treat him at once.

Luckily the nail had not gone in too deep and she was able to pull it out with no problem. It had only left a little hole in his head which she treated and bandaged and gave him a tetanus shot. The nail had been new, fortunately, not rusty and did not penetrate too far. I did not ever notice any subsequent scar on his beautiful little face, but Ken says he has a small scar on his head. I thought it was Neil who was involved in this accident, but, on reading an early draft of this memoir, Ken said it must have been him. He did not remember anything about it but it explained that small scar.

At this stage I would like to introduce my family.

DAD

Coral to Daddy at war

Dad was tall and slim and had dark wavy hair. He was, all bias aside, a very good looking man. He had still a good head of hair with little grey when he died. He rarely, if ever, swore nor did he drink alcohol.

He did like his smoke however and he rolled his own for the most part and would take some time, each night, to roll up his supply for the next day, placing them in an appropriate tin. Dad was in pain a lot of the time, being plagued with sinusitis along with a very painful headache, almost like a migraine. When it struck it would have him in bed for some time, unable to stand the light or any noise.

Dad had malaria during the war, as he spent a lot of those years in New Guinea. I understand that the disease came back with some symptoms for many years afterwards.

Another of Dad's health problems was a bad back. At one stage, not only was he in very much pain, but he had a large area on his leg where the hair did not grow and was numb. Apparently the discs were pressing on his spine and cutting off the circulation. Dad had an operation to correct this problem, but spent six months literally flat on his back. Once on his feet again, he was required to wear a stiff brace. The pain, subsequently, was very little relieved.

Despite his health problems, Dad had a wonderful dry wit and you had to keep your wits about you on talking to him, as he would come back with a dry funny remark which would have us all laughing.

This wonderful humorous trait was, thankfully passed down to my elder son Tony.

Our home was always loving and happy and an ideal place to grow up.

One occasion, which I will always remember as an example of that love and wit, began with Mum and I doing something together in the kitchen, and Dad coming in and making some cheeky comment to Mum. Her reply was, jokingly and with a smile in her voice "Go put your head in a bag!" A phrase I had heard many times before from those same lips. Dad went out and Mum and I got on with our chores, taking no notice of what else was happening. On hearing a quiet voice say "How's this then?" We turned around and there stood Dad with, can you guess? A hessian bag pulled over his head!

Well it's a wonder anyone got any tea that night as we almost laughed our heads off and, of course, not being able to resist passing the joke on to my brothers, had another round of laughs when they came in. I think Dad would have thought he had got his money's worth out of this one!

He was very reticent to speak about the years he spent up in Papua New Guinea. He had a hole which I thought was maybe a bullet hole in his arm. There was no talk of him being wounded, however, and I don't recall anyone saying how long he was there. He brought home a lot of things he had made when up there.

One thing with which I was enthralled was a collection of beautiful butterflies. They were mounted on boards on which the butterflies were nestled in cotton wool. The whole thing was then covered with thin Perspex.

The most beautiful one of them all was one about four to five inches, wide tip to tip of its wings and about two inches tall. It was the most beautiful deep blue and, if I recall, was called a 'Swallow Tail'. All the butterflies were very beautiful. There were two boards with about six to eight butterflies on each. I vaguely remember someone saying it may have been illegal to collect butterflies from New Guinea.

The butterflies sadly have all crumbled to dust now, as have both Mum and Dad, so guess there's no harm done now.

Dad also had a ring and bits of other jewellery that he had made from aluminium taken from crashed aircraft. He also made leather articles like plaited belts, a hand bag and more, all made with embossed work on them.

There were a few other things which I can't remember now. I guess they had a bit of spare time up there with nothing to do.

He did not see me, his first child, until I was eighteen months old. Dad had been sent away in 1942 before I was born and did not return until the end of the war. I have photos that Mum had sent him with 'To Daddy, with love' written on the back. It must have been so difficult and heartbreaking to have your husband away for so long.

In addition to him being away, it must have been even worse not to have your husband there when your first child was born. Mum spent the war years prior to and after my birth with her mother in Geelong. This was why I was born in Geelong.

Dad spoke lovingly of the 'Fuzzy-Wuzzy Angels' as all the Australian soldiers called the natives of Papua New Guinea. He said they had saved many Australian soldiers, carrying and leading the wounded to safety, hiding them and helping them through the jungles and mud bogs. He often called a cup of tea 'Kai-kai', as it was called there, and had an odd word here and there he had learned from them. He said the Fuzzy-Wuzzies had a wonderful nature.

Dad worked on an asparagus farm at some stage down Geelong way before the war. He knew the best way to grow them, and that the most delectable part was the white stalks, kept underground to keep the sun off them. It is rare to see asparagus for sale like this but the gourmet chefs know and demand them for their dishes.

He had a special asparagus picker. It had a long handle and a flat wider end which you pushed right down into the ground and cut the asparagus quite a few inches underground.

During the depression it was difficult to get work and we lived off the land with Dad taking any job available, if any.

When I was first going to school, Dad was working at the Ezard's Saw Mill and he rode his push bike to work, having clips on his trousers to keep them out of the chain and a very fetching beret on his head to keep the sawdust out.

I do not remember seeing anyone else wearing a beret, but I remember Mum buying his in Bairnsdale and I don't think they were very scarce. Since then I have seen a photo of him and his workmates with others wearing berets. I always understood that the beret was a French man's hat.

The farm work was shared by us all, including Dad, despite has bad back.

He was taken too soon at 53 years old. He had motor neuron disease. This was apparently rife in New Guinea at the time he was there, but the army did not admit that he would have contracted it there and that it would have caused his death. Mum was unable to get a war-widow's pension. In spite of the fact that Dad's brother did not leave Australia, his wife received a full such pension.

This disease was a wasting disease which affected all his muscles, starting with his arms so that he had trouble doing his hair. It also always sounded as if he had a cold. Later, he was unable to use his muscles to swallow or even breathe and was unable to talk to us. He made light of these problems even after his diagnosis. He told no-one until the disease was well advanced. He then told my husband and, I later found out, a family friend, neither of whom broke his confidence. I still miss my dearest Dad.

Now we come to Mum.

MUM

I'd like you to get to know Lavinia Ethel Boucher, nee Barnes.

I could never completely describe the many wonderful traits which existed in this strong and loving lady who was known as 'Ven' to her family, Auntie Neenie to her nieces and nephews, grandma to her grandchildren and great grandma to her doting great-grandchildren

Her love for all her children and their partners, grandchildren and great grand-children was all encompassing. Mum was one of nine children and there was not (as she would often say) time or money to spoil any of them. She, along with the other older children, was expected to help with the younger ones and to help with house cleaning.

Mum was a beautiful person both physically and within her soul.

She was not as shy and retiring as Dad but not nearly so outgoing as her sister. Mum had been a maid in a big house in Geelong and was taught the correct way to carry out the many domestic duties, a skill she would not need too much of in her early days in the bush.

She was very efficient and taught me all she had learned. Although she spent many hours on the farm and in the garden, she always kept a very happy, clean and well-run house.

Mum and her sister and Mum's mother if she was visiting, used to walk to church pushing babies in prams with other children tagging behind. In the winter-time they each wore their fox-skin stoles. They wore them around their shoulders. They must have been quite warm. It was a real fox-skin with the beady eyes and mouth holding onto the brush (tail). I would never touch it as those beady eyes and sharp teeth would frighten me,

She was secretary for the C.W.A, secretary and treasurer for the Ladies Guild, President of the School Council and involved in many organizations every year for the school and church fetes

Mum would be busy for many weeks beforehand, cooking and packing sweets, and almost any kind you could think of. She made toffee apples and nearer the time the biscuits and slices and in the last few days, cakes both large and small. For ages before the fete, every available surface would be covered in trays, boxes and tins full of her work. These could be anything from seedlings to ripe vegetables which were gathered from the vegetable garden also.

The day before the fete Mum would be out in the garden, preparing seedlings for sale and gathering the pots of cuttings she had previously taken. Then, early on the morning of the fete, Mum would be out in the garden once more. This time she would be picking huge bunches of flowers and putting them in buckets of water.

It was all hands on deck to load the car and trailer with the bounty. I'm sure it would have required more than one trip to town to get everything there.

I don't know how much she would take on her stall but it would have been a decent amount to add to the other money from other stallholders for their fund raising effort. This might have been a once-a-year donation of time and produce from Mum for each of the two organizations.

However, this occasion gives just an inkling of Mum's great giving heart.

In addition to that was Harvest Thanksgiving at the church. As many people as were able would donate produce from the garden, orchards and farms to celebrate thanksgiving. As you would imagine, my Mum and Dad would be involved in all of this, showing our thankfulness for the harvest of our crops.

Some night shortly after the harvest festival Sunday, an auction would be held for goods which had been donated.

This was held in the church and was a very social occasion

One person that always comes to my mind was a fairly portly man, a cousin of Dads. He would sit in his corner with his hands resting on his well-fed tummy and he would always start off the bidding with 'Four bob!' followed by a real belly-laugh, his hands jumping up and down on his tummy.

Everyone would watch for his 'Four bob' bid and laugh so much that bidding would cease for a short while until everyone, including 'Four Bob' had contained themselves.

Mum's hair began turning grey at sixteen and I can always remember her as greying. As she grew older, her hair became a beautiful snow white.

Mum's greatest love was her garden; she would be out weeding the day after coming home from hospital after an operation. She did it automatically and couldn't stop herself. Mum always said she not only grew a beautiful garden for herself but also for passers-by. She would always have compliments on her garden wherever she lived.

Mum would go out each morning to see which new flower had come out. Often I would try to beat her to it, but I think there was only once, except when she was sick in bed, that I was able to tell her of a new blooming flower before she had seen it herself.

We would often find a teapot or saucepan sitting on a post outside.

Mum would have gone to empty the teapot in the garden, or take out scraps for the chooks and get engrossed in weeding or communing with her garden and had forgotten about the pot outside. She would often come in with a pinny full of tomatoes or fruit or whatever happened to be ripe.

It was quite common for Mum to say "I don't know where that saucepan is". This would trigger a hunt out in the garden by all of us to find the missing pot.

Even on her ninetieth birthday, just a couple of days before she was taken, although she was in a coma and unable to see the flowers which just thronged her room, I described and named all the flowers for her, believing she could hear. My sister in law remarked on how well she had taught me to be able to do that. I still appreciate the love of flowers and gardens she inspired in me.

Mum was always enthusiastic about anything her children, and later her grandchildren, would undertake and achieve. She always supported us in whatever we attempted.

She would always think of others ahead of herself. You wouldn't dare mention something you might like as she always made an attempt to get it for us. When I was having trouble with my joints in my early days of marriage, she bought me an electric blanket for our bed as she considered it would help. We were not very solvent in those days, but neither was she.

Mum seemed to be the disciplinarian in our home especially with me, but I can recall only two times when I was given the strap.

The first I can recall was when, as a young girl, perhaps seven or eight, I had torn my knickers on a blackberry bush. They were badly torn and I didn't think they were any good, so I threw them on the rubbish tip, which was an old gold mining hole.

But didn't the fur fly when I arrived home without them. I was given the strap and sent to my room and had to stay there without any food for the rest of the day.

At the time, I did not consider the crime merited the punishment, but as I grew older I understood Mum's reason for her drastic actions. I could understand that, for one, there would be little spare money in the house and Mum could have mended the garment very easily. They were irretrievable in this big hole with blackberries, snakes and many years of rubbish to contend with.

The other reason I now understand would be her young daughter coming home with no knickers after playing with cousins, both boys and girls. It would be a shock for her with that thought in her mind. This I would not have known about in those days due to my naivety.

The second time that I can recall such punishment was when I came home from school with a hole in my shoes. Mum belted me with the shoe saying how I was always hard on shoes. Once again I was sent to my room with no food. I understand now that the economic side of things would come into play. Mum was probably worrying about how she would get the money for another pair.

There was also the added expense of a sixty-odd mile round trip to Bairnsdale, which did not happen very often. The injustice I felt was that the shoes were second hand when I got them. And free at that. But the situation at the time was this: We had another family living with us because their house had burnt down. I don't know where we all fitted. I am not sure how long they stayed, but we had the stress of additional people, the couple and at least one extra child in the house,

The extra cooking and the additional goods required to feed them would all add to assist with the rise in mum's blood pressure. All this also showed the kindness of my mother's heart and there were many more instances of her unselfishness.

Mum had a beautiful singing voice and often sang at weddings in our church and at many special occasions. Her brother Gern also had a wonderful voice and she was always rapt to hear him sing

Towards the end of her life, we found many Readers' Digest books and Videos. They would have been very expensive but I'm sure she had bought them for one of her children or grandchildren for birthday or Christmas presents ready for when we came. But we didn't come and they were stacked up there sometimes duplicated where she had bought one and forgotten she had bought it. Another reason for the many products was that you had to place an order to enter their sweepstakes which was for quite a large sum of money. Once again this was for us. She kept trying to win some money to help us out.

It's very sad the number of elderly people waiting at home for loved ones to turn up and they don't. Often the younger people would have jobs and responsibilities and be unable to go and see them.

In some cases people don't care enough. In the case of our family, distance, work and responsibilities and other things would be the problem, not the lack of love. Mum was always thinking of us and was always so unselfish.

She battled through her illnesses and even towards the end was so frustrated that, no matter what she did, or how hard she tried she could not get on top of her problem and bounce back as she had always previously done. She was a very strong and tough lady but always so loving. She was always a lady in spite of her rough life and I don't remember ever hearing a single swear word from her.

I was in Traralgon, enjoying my role of grandma to two of my grandchildren when she was diagnosed with cancer. After a major operation, and a long stay in hospital, she was able to go home. She was given weak doses of chemo in tablet form and she thought she had beaten it. Unfortunately it got the better of her and she was forced to go into a nursing home. I begged her to come and live with me many times, but, knowing my health was not good, she refused. I think she wanted to stay close to my brothers. It broke my heart for me to tell her, after a family conference, that she would have to go into a nursing home as she was unable to cope alone. The very thought of her loneliness and unhappiness still affects me. My brother Ken was very good and visited her almost every day, making a long round trip after work. Ken and Julie had always been very good to her and she idolized them.

If I had known how little time she actually had I would have organized my responsibilities at Traralgon and gone down to stay with her, if she would have allowed it. I really think she was in the best place for her at that time.

We had gone down to see her one weekend as they said she was very low, and after visiting her, on our way back to Mum's place my brother rang me. He said he had bad news and I thought Mum had gone. However, it was her sister who had had a major haemorrhage and passed on. We did not tell Mum of Auntie's passing as she was in a coma and we didn't want to distress her.

She, I'm sure, determinedly hung on until her birthday and then slipped away just two days later. I will always remember when Ken rang me to say she had gone. A physical pain went through my heart. I now believe a heart can break. After he hung up I howled like a dingo, then after pulling myself together, I thought of the weeping and wailing we see in other countries. I hoped I had not woken the neighbours.

Ken was very, very good then with informing her relatives and friends and reading the eulogy. He was the rock which my younger brother and my children and I clung to. She lost her battle after determinedly reaching ninety years of age.

We will always remember and adore our wonderful mother, grandmother and great grandmother.

KEN

Now it's Kenneth that I want you to know. As he was five years younger, I can't remember much about Ken in his boyhood other than to say that he was always a deep thinker, a very hard worker and always helping at whatever job needed doing.

I recall I always played Mother's-helper, changing, dressing, bathing and feeding him. He used to tease me very often when we were children, which was the cause of many fights between us then. However, we all loved each other dearly.

Ken has grown into the most loving, caring man. He is very quiet and unassuming and he reminds me of my mum's brother Gernard as he is always thinking of others. Ken is a real perfectionist and he worries away at something until he gets it right.

This is very evident in his coffee making. He trained as a Barista and in his own business, was always working to perfect his coffee, even to the extent of worrying about the taste of the milk at certain times of the year. All this paid off as his coffee was chosen as the best available in Geelong.

Ken worked in radio as a cameraman and in television. He then progressed to a position as news—reader and then on to being the manager of a television station.

After some time working for others, he became disillusioned with the working for wages system.

He married a wonderful girl called Julie who was ideal for him, being most hard-working, ambitious and capable. Ken and Julie bought a newsagent-cafe type shop in Melbourne and after working very hard with very long hours, having only one or two half-days off in a year, they built the business up into a thriving concern. They eventually were able to sell it at a profit and move on.

Somewhere along the way they had two lovely little boys making their days much longer. Mum was quick to help out in looking after the boys and was willing to assist in whatever respect was necessary.

Ken and Julie then bought a 'Pure and Natural' cafe franchise in Geelong, and later, a second such business. Once again they were working very hard, long hours with Ken always thinking how to improve the business. This resulted in them being named the best 'Pure and Natural' business not only in this state, but other states as well. They then after some time opened another such shop in Geelong. Now they had one in each of the large shopping plazas.

Eventually, realising that they were only working to pay the staff which had increased greatly, along with superannuation and sick pay and staff problems, they decided to sell. They operated only one business for a while and finally sold at a price far less than the value of each. Afterwards, with Julie working for others for a while, they bought into a one man business in Geelong. After building this business up to having a large staff and extending the shop, they again sold but never for what it was worth.

They had thought of retiring as Ken had been battling health problems for many years, but found they needed to keep themselves busy. Julie now works for someone else and is really enjoying it and helping to improve that business. Ken now works a few hours per week as Barista at their old shop. They now have time to follow their beloved 'Cats'.

When in their different shops in Geelong, several of the Geelong players would come in for a coffee, lunch etc. They got to know some of them very well. In the earlier days, they sponsored one of the players who was just a rookie. The player became captain of the team and has since retired and is a much respected businessman in Geelong.

I will always remember how very wonderful Ken was with Mum in her later years. He was always loving and thoughtful, always considerate of her and doing all he could to help.

To earn some extra money I cleaned the local Bank and attached residence once a week. It made for a busy life for me, but I remained cheerful and happy with my lot and was always pleased to leave a clean house behind me. One later manager always had frayed sleeve cuffs and he or his wife trimmed the fraying edges to make them look tidier. Later, on learning the managers' salaries, I could see why.

Even though the bank manager was supposed to be a king-pin in the town, I was surprised his salary was rather small compared with those of others. He had two children I think. It would have been worse had he had a larger family.

Although our salaries weren't too big comparatively, the tellers were told to smarten themselves up with new shirts, ties and jumpers. This would be a drain on their budgets. We girls were issued with a uniform. I can't remember if we had to pay for them. The one I liked most was an aqua colour with white collars which could be removed and washed each day. We had one other collar to clip on in its place.

These would be washed. blued and starched and fastened to the uniform fresh each day. I believe I had two to interchange. The belt was made from self-material with buttons to fasten it. The sleeves were long and the skirt was lightly gored. Another less popular colour was a dull dark greyish-blue in the same pattern. I was glad when that one was replaced.

My most exciting day was when a teller told me I should enter the Miss Australia Quest as he thought I looked a bit like Tania Verstock who was a title holder about that time. I was very flattered but I thought that his girlfriend, who was my best friend, would be a better prospect.

He scoffed and I responded, "How could I do that in a little town like this?"

It was a real compliment and would give me a lift for quite a while afterwards even though I did not believe that I had looks that were in anyway special.

NEIL

Now comes Neil, who is six years younger than Ken.

Once again, I cannot recall a lot about Neil as a child. I remember going into town and wheeling Neil around in his pram. Many people would stop me and say what a beautiful baby he was. Some often remarked to Mum how the Bouchers made beautiful babies. I know I looked after him a lot when he was young, feeding him, bathing him, changing his nappies and generally playing the little mother.

He had beautiful blonde curls and we were all very sorry when they had to be cut off. He was the lucky one out of us three to retain his curls to this day, although not in his opinion of course! Just like my son with lovely curly hair. They had to have it cut to get rid of the curls. How envious the girls were.

Because he was so much younger, he was not involved in our early adventures. He was also a hard worker and helped with any tasks we were involved in. Neil was and still is also a deep thinker and remains the shyest amongst us all. He is also very easy going, thoughtful and loving. I saw less of Neil as I was married when he was nine and I was working for several years before then. Mum, Dad and Neil left Swift's Creek when he was about twelve years old.

When Neil left school, he went into the Roads Board and worked there for many years until deciding it was a dead-end job. He realised that he would be waiting for someone to die before gaining a promotion. Neil then joined the Police force and did very well there.

I remember how very proud Mum was at his graduation parade, we all were. It was a thrilling event. The new graduates were all marching across the parade ground with everyone in step, their brand new uniforms making a striking picture. All of them stood with shoulders back, chests out and looking very proud of themselves. During the march past, they saluted a senior officer in the Force.

Coral Neil and Ken at Neil Police graduation

The music was rousing and most appropriate for the day. After the march past we all went inside and were treated to a delicious afternoon tea with the cream cakes, sponges, chocolate éclairs and imaginative finger food a great temptation. We all agreed that as we had very rarely been treated to such a delectable spread, we should all make the most of it.

Neil worked in Melbourne on the beat in some very rough areas. Although he didn't say much about it, I do remember him saying how tough it was chasing crooks, jumping over back fences and along back alleys.

Neil gained promotion to Sergeant and eventually took command of several one-man stations one at a time over several years. Having married, he then had two beautiful children and he was posted to Werribee, bought a nice house and settled in for a while. He went to University at night to gain a degree in I.T. He gained a further degree and at last he resigned from the Force.

Jan, his wife, said it was a nightmare being a policeman's wife, always imagining a knock at the door and one of his colleagues saying that he had lost his life to a crook's bullet or to any of the dangers they faced. We always said Neil was too soft at heart to be a policeman.

Considering the horrific accidents and other events he had to witness, often going to the home of the victim to tell the parents of their child's death, it must have been horrific.

Mum of course worried about him too as he was her 'baby boy'.

The stress eventually got too much for him and he moved on and obtained very good jobs within the computer industry. He worked his way up until he was working in the role of a 'trouble shooter'. When there was a problem, he was expected to fix it. Once again the stress became too much and he put in many applications for other jobs.

However, he was considered too highly qualified for most of the positions.

Eventually he obtained his 'dream job' which involved not having to travel through peak hour traffic, was closer to his home and much less stressful.

He moved on and after some years, one of his previous bosses begged him to go back. After much consideration he agreed but, as luck would have it, that business crashed during the crisis within that industry.

He was out of a job for quite a long time and found himself once again too highly qualified. Also, he was not as young as before. Neil became very despondent at being out of work for so long that he would have worked at anything. He has now obtained a job again in the computer industry and is much happier.

Neil was also an avid orchid grower, winning prizes in many different shows for numerous years. He was an office bearer for an orchid club in that area for some years. It was fascinating going to their home and seeing orchids everywhere in the house.

I loved, and still do, all flowers but orchids held a special place in my heart, perhaps because I was unable to grow them in Swift's Creek because of the severe frosts. I later erected a greenhouse to protect a few. However, I still had to have kerosene lanterns and fans in there to keep them alive in winter. A shade-house in summer also helped, but I was never able to grow them to Neil's standard.

Neil also grew African Violets for years and made me jealous once again having battled to grow them. He had great success with these until a disease, carried in from soil from a pot brought into his collection wiped out the lot.

Neil took up photography somewhere around this time. He attended classes and once again was very successful, going to the U.S. for a short time to further his studies with his tutor, who was a very highly respected photographer over there. He became an excellent photographer, creating calendars with copies of his photographs. He was very highly regarded amongst his fellow photographers.

He made up prints and framed them to sell on the internet and also did some wedding photography, which was really beautiful. Neil would have loved to become a professional photographer. Unfortunately he lacked the confidence, as he says to 'sell' his work and himself.

I wish I had the skill to help people believe in themselves. There are many, many people out there who would benefit from this. Neil did not believe in himself enough to do what was required. But then, having said that, I don't even have confidence in myself!

There are too many of us out there who are too shy to put themselves forward. There is a niche for many, many 'someone's' to help people believe in themselves without it costing them very much. So there, 'Mr Multimillionaire' is an excellent idea for someone to set up a program of learning to teach those who need it to increase their belief in themselves. I know that there are such programs out there already but they cost a great deal of money. Such a program should be set up at a very minimal cost and be easily available to those who need it.

I believe that the good schools now make some effort to instil this sort of self confidence in their young students. Perhaps children, even in the Bush, are taught to believe in themselves these days.

So there readers, you have a brief verbal picture of my family. From this, I'm sure you can see how very proud I am of them all and how I love them.

JURHIM

My aunt and uncle lived next to us in the house they called 'Jurhim' (an amalgamation of letters taken from the childrens' names).

They were a very close family to us as the two brothers married the two sisters and they felt almost like second parents to us. The girls I considered as my sisters as I had no others and the boy as an older brother. We did everything together.

We all made amusements for ourselves. We had dug a cave into the side of a mine working behind their house. We spent a long time there and it was our 'cubby house' for a while.

There was an immensely beautiful tree just past their place on the track leading down to the creek. It had beautiful branches stretching up towards the sky and the huge strong trunk was mottled with many shades of brown. This provided a home for a myriad of birds, insects and animals. For some reason we spent a lot of time there, sipping at the sweet nectar of the mistletoe flowers and vying with the honeyeaters and bees that lived on that delectable tasting treat. The Mistletoe having attached itself in several big bunches on the branches of the tree kept the honey makers busy.

The eldest girl, June was younger than her brother and I. She was, and still is, a very sweet little girl, petite and brown eyed with not a lot to say for herself. But wind her up too far, and she would spit fire. She had a slight lisp and one occasion always comes to mind. The lisp meant that her 'S's' came out as a'Sh'.

On this particular day, she saw a small piece of tin on the track and said "I'm going to sit on this" But with her lisp, the 'S' came out with a different meaning! Being a well brought up family, we did not swear and perhaps this was why it was so amusing that that would come out of the mouth of little June. Her sister, Rhonda, was younger than her and was almost Ken's age. She was involved in all our games. For some reason, I cannot recall Rhonda doing anything in particular but she was always taking part in our many adventures.

Rhonda became a nurse and was head of a large children's ward in a big Geelong hospital. She was a very caring and loving girl.

This family left Swift's Creek to move back to Geelong to provide better schooling for the children. Jim progressed over the years to Head Inspector for Schools in Victoria, so their move proved successful. With my aunt and uncle both gone, I rarely see my cousins now, which is a shame. Many of my cousins went onto high level positions in their careers which showed how good schooling made a difference.

Dad's first cousin's children were a case in point. Trevor Boucher was Deputy Commissioner for Taxation and his brother in an equally prestigious position.

Mum's brother's boy reached a high level in the Reserve Bank and drove around in a Porsche. One other cousin is a pilot with Quantas and his sister an air hostess. There are many other success stories in my family but time and space do not permit me to list them all.

DAD'S BIG SHED

Dad built a very large shed on high stumps, in the paddock on the top side of the house. In this he stored his tools and built his many projects for the house and toys for the boys. One reason for the high stumps was to, hopefully, keep the mice out. These crafty little creatures seem to find their way past any obstacles.

Apples and mainly apricots were sliced in half and put out on the frames to dry and taken into the large shed, still on the frames, at night or during wet weather.

WALNUTS

At the appropriate time of the year, walnuts from the many trees on the property were spread out in single layers on the wooden floor. These were set out to dry the top skin on the nut to allow it to be removed easily.

These walnuts were delicious as were any fruit, nuts and vegetables taken straight from the source. They were used in baking—cakes, biscuits, slices and sweets such as toffee for the fetes which were always more tasty when fresh walnuts were added. This nut was even tastier when roasted in the coals of an open fire

One thing that would make Mum very cross was that the majority of our nut trees were in a line further up the road from our place, near a wattle daub cottage. If the cottage was empty at the time, Mum would hear a car stop on the road further up, just above these trees. Mum would race up there in an attempt to stop them taking the nuts, but it was a bit of a trek and Mum was no Olympic runner. The people would have got back to their car and be taking off as she got there. They had been stealing the walnuts. She hated people stealing fruit etc. She would give them away to anyone who actually asked, and to some hard up people, but could not stomach theft.

Another use for walnuts, not widely known, is to chop them and then put them with chopped dates and a little butter. Mash this together and, warm or cold, it is delectable on a scone or bread and used for fillings in cakes and slices. Delicious!

One task which was so boring was to crack the walnuts, leaving only the shelled nut intact. The nuts were cracked with a hammer, putting only the kernel in the jar and leaving the shells in the paper on which they had been spread.

This was a job always given to Scouts, Brownies, Cubs and Guides when they came for Bob-a-Job. This was one way in which they would raise money, either for charity or for equipment. The Bob-a-Job was just a name for the practice each year, when householders or shopkeepers were required to pay a bob (shilling) for any job done.

Sometimes people would take advantage and give them a job worth much more. The job set at our place was to fill a large jar of cracked nuts for the money.

If the job was done more quickly and more nuts were cracked, a few more pennies would be paid.

The Girl Guide or other such trouper would have their card signed and the money paid. This was taken back to the Troup and there was always a bit of competition as to who would raise the most money. We always looked forward to seeing the Bob-a-Jobbers and welcomed them all because we used many walnuts in our baking.

Dad and most other men were able to crack the nuts, one against the other, in their hand. One type of walnut was a much larger nut with a softer shell. They would be much in demand. We would sell the nuts to anyone wanting them. Many went on the stalls for the fetes and harvest festivals. We would find walnuts on the ground, chewed into by mice (which must have had very strong teeth) and the possums, which helped themselves to a great number.

CHOIR

At Mum's funeral, Ken, in the eulogy, said how Mum had a beautiful voice and had thankfully passed it on to their sister Coral, who is me of course.

Talking about it later, my brothers both said that they hadn't been given the talent and my sisters-in-law said they wished they could sing, and what was I doing with it?

Feeling very guilty at not using my voice for many years, I hunted around, phoned and asked around to find some way for me to sing.

I was offered a position (voluntarily) of choir leader if I would start up a choir for one group. I did not feel I had enough experience in that kind of work. I eventually, after being given phone number and being passed on to another, found a group who were looking for singers. The group was meeting that week and I was asked to go along.

I actually, unknowingly turned up as they were practising for their annual concert. I said, as I hadn't practised with them, that I would sing at practice but not take part in the concert. As it happened I knew all the songs but one and the choir leader said I was an asset to the choir and she wanted me to take part in the concert. This was the Elderly citizen's choir in Morwell and I sang with them for many years.

It was shortly after starting with the first choir I was told of another choir who were looking for singers. I went along and was asked to join. This was the C.W.A choir in Morwell. I sang also with that choir for some years and when they amalgamated to become 'Friends in Song'.

Even though I had sung solo many times and in front of large crowds, I was extremely nervous when asked to sing solo just in front of the choir. I was so nervous and I was shaking so much for a half-hour later. The choir leader said if I was that nervous perhaps I had better not sing solo. Eventually I did lose some of my nerves and sang solo for a verse or with another singer. I sang with that choir until my back did not allow me to stand long enough to sing a full bracket.

I left the choir for twelve months and then, my health having improved, I went to hear them sing at their annual concert. All I wanted to do was get up there and sing with them. It brought tears to my eyes hearing those sweet voices. I asked the choir leader if I could join them for the Christmas Carol program where they sang Carols in nursing homes each week.

That choir had a reputation for being very good and we were asked to sing by the City Council at the opening of elderly citizen's week.

Having joined them for the Carols' program, I returned and continued with them until my health forced me to permanently give it up. I still miss it very much. I made some very good friends in that choir and two of them still visit me and keep in touch.

Bless you J and T. Look after yourselves, love you.

WATTLE & DAUB COTTAGE

The wattle & daub cottage was made of frames with wire-netting stretched over them and then mud thrown against it. This would require several layers and was then painted with whitewash.

In one room was a bullock's blood floor. The mud was mixed with bullock's blood to stabilise the mixture. It was smoothed off and I'm not sure if the blood was the top coat but it had a dark red glaze and was hard as though it had been finished off with lacquer.

It did not smell badly, as you would expect it to. You could wipe it over with a damp cloth. This cottage was habitable and was leased to tenants for a long time.

In the orchard behind this cottage were several apple trees, the fruit of which had a beautiful flavour. The Snow Apple, one of the old heritage apples, was delicious. It had a pure snowy-white flesh and was crunchy and sweet. The fruit was not very big, but it had never had the benefit of any water or feeding probably since it was planted in the gold-mining days.

There were several gooseberry bushes, not the kiwi fruit or Chinese Gooseberry but the true berry bush which I have never seen before or since. The bushes were only about a half-meter tall and you needed to be careful when picking to avoid the spikes. The fruit was bigger than a cherry, but a translucent light green and was very tasty once completely ripe. It was a bit tart but had a flavour all of its own.

There was also a large plot of asparagus which we were all very fond of. Asparagus grew wild along the creeks and rivers and in Bruthen, along the railway line.

Further up along the river were other mine workings, not shafts, unless they had fallen in, but a big open area of quite deep diggings. On scrabbling around in there, as we did, we found a shelf dug into the wall of the diggings and partly buried. On it was a tin box. It looked like the shelf had been made to accommodate the box.

I think we had to dig a bit to find it. The tin box was about three inches deep and eighteen inches square. When we first found it, we thought we had found a fortune in cash or gold. We squealed and danced around in excitement. But it was empty. What a disappointment, we were shattered. The dreams of gold nuggets and big houses and flash cars came to an abrupt halt. We continued on with our search with hope for another day.

SWIMMING HOLE

Just below these diggings was a favourite swimming hole because it was quite deep and had a large rock from which we could dive or lay on and sun-bake.

Just above this area, on the other side of the road, was our 'cubby-house'. It was made from just five or so saplings which had grown in a square or rough circle, also having a small bit of Ti-Tree scrub which made an enclosure. It became our little room to play 'pretend' in.

Over the road in cows' paddock was a mine shaft and just around the corner and below the road, were two others. We didn't enter any of those but I remember seeing, later on, that one had caved in. So they really were unsafe.

INSECTS

The usual blow-flies and house-flies were annoying, but the March Flies gave a nasty sting when they bit our damp skin after swimming. They also used to bite the cows at that time too.

The mud wasp would make us wary as they looked so dangerous. They were orange and black and fairly large. They used to collect mud from around a puddle and take it off to build their distinctive mud nests.

The Bull Ant could pack a wallop and you would certainly know if one had bitten you. They were a big ant, bigger than the Sugar Ant which was the same shade of brown but normally did not bite, unless you stood on their nest. Then they got a bit angry. Their bites did not leave any after-effects.

The Bluebottle, a large shiny bluey/green colour was also said to be very lethal and we always steered clear of them. The Jack Jumpers I have described in another section and they are very dangerous for some people. The little brown beetles were a pest as they got onto the white clothes on the line and white flowers, making a mess with brown spots everywhere.

The dung beetles did the clean-up work by rolling the dung into large balls and dragging them into their holes. This was also effective in fertilizing the land.

The Christmas Beetles were a large beetle in iridescent colours which appeared around Christmas time. I'm sorry to say the boys delighted in hitting them with a tennis racquet. Then there were the moths and butterflies which are known almost everywhere in Australia. The Flood Moth or Dargo Moth was a large brown moth about two and a half inches across. They belted themselves against the windows at night wanting to get to the light. One other insect which I was afraid of was the gnat. It would come inside to the light at night and looked dangerous with its orange and black colouring. When they bit it was very painful and they usually bit more than once as they tended to get inside your clothes.

They were usually dispatched with a shoe or some other handy implement. The spiders were many and probably widespread and well-known and all greatly feared by me.

The harlequin bugs were always a thing of amusement as they used attach themselves to each other, end to end and make a living black and yellow train.

The scorpions, earwigs and centipedes were all said to be poisonous.

WILD ANIMALS

During our wonderful roaming times around there, we would often come across some of nature's little friends. Not so friendly, to our thinking, were the snakes. We were warned never to go near them, to just let them go past, and tell an adult if it was close to the house. In those days, snakes were greatly feared and if one was found near a house the adults would attempt to kill it. This was not illegal in those days. When one was killed it was put onto an anthill. The ants would soon take care of it and would have it all eaten up within a few days.

Another friend we would come across was the echidna or porcupine. We once had one at home and tried to keep it for a pet. I don't know how it came to be there as we would never pick one up for fear of the thorns. Perhaps it just wandered in. It wasn't a success as a pet as it would always have burrowed down into the ground and under the netting or whatever we tried to keep it in. Thank goodness we were unable to tame this wonderful native creature, as we would not have known what to feed it, and it would have been so cruel. We did not think of such things in those days.

The platypus was said to live with its family a little way up the creek. I was never lucky enough to see it.

We very rarely saw a wombat around the houses but they were in evidence further up the creek. The kangaroos and wallabies were usually higher up the hills. Rabbits were around in abundance and foxes too. Emus were to be seen quite often but rare enough to be a novelty.

A group of kangaroos would gather on a piece of flat land across the creek. We had been told stories of how the kangaroo, after being harassed by a dog would drag it to the water and drown it. Other stories were told of kangaroos boxing the dogs as if in a boxing ring, then stand on its great strong tail, and rip the dog's belly from top to bottom. If we had any dogs with us, we made sure to keep them near us.

Ken remembers going with his uncle whistling foxes. There was a bounty at that time on foxes because there were so many of them and they were killing lambs and even fowls. A complete flock could be wiped out overnight if a fox got into the pen. Once you had shot the fox, you took it, or part of it, into the Land Department office and were paid money for your trouble.

Fox traps were also set, but facing a snarling, vicious wounded fox in a trap was one thing I would never want to experience again. The hairs on the back of my neck would stand up to mimic those of the fox and its mouth agape full of sharp teeth sent shivers up my spine. Its eyes spat sparks and a growl back in its throat would send me running.

Ken, during our talks about life at "Emoh Rou" recalled many hours spent roaming the hills 'whistling 'foxes. The whistles were made from a piece of tin, cut into a certain shape and a hole drilled in it. When the whistle was put into your mouth and blown through it, it would sound like a rabbit squealing, which brought the fox running. One could buy a fox whistle of course, but why would you?

In the cleared area coming down out of the wooded hills, you could see a fox weaving its way around bushes, stumps and small hills coming towards you with its very fine brush waving above him. Sometimes it was only this bushy tail we could see as it crept through long grass and low scrub. I, for one, would feel the hairs standing up on the back of my neck as it came closer. I knew it would run for its life when it saw us, and I also knew we were in no danger. Even so, it <u>was</u> a wild animal.

Another friend we had was the Blue Tongue lizard. There always seemed to be one there in the garden somewhere. We were told that he ate the slugs and snails so we left him alone. You would always know there was one there when the pet dog kicked up a fuss, yapping and carrying on. The dog had a distinctive bark when he had a Blue Tongue rounded up. Perhaps he thought it might be a snake.

WILD FLOWERS

Other wondrous things we found in days as bush kids were the wild flowers which would bloom in the spring. These were not as prolific as the ones which can be seen in Western Australia, but equally is beautiful in their own way.

The first one which comes to mind is the 'Snake Flower'. We had been told it was always to be seen when and where there was a snake about.

Whilst we loved the cyclamen pink of the dainty little flowers all the way up a long stem, roughly two feet high, rising from a base of thick, short leaves, we usually admired it from a distance. I believe it grew from a bulb in the ground. It may have been a trigger plant. But I'm sure someone will put me right.

The next wild flower beauty was the Bluebell. A beautiful blue bell on stems about eight inches high. These grew in a thicker clump than the Snake Flower but were still quite sparse.

The Yellow Bell was another much rarer flower in that area.

The Dandelion, as we called it as children, was a lovely bright daisy. These were not found in the bush so much but in more cleared areas. They make a wonderful cheery sight and we loved to make daisy-chains with them as well as wear them on our heads

The highly perfumed Boronia was found in higher mountain areas but not in our little valley. The wild clematis made a striking picture as it climbed all over surrounding trees. The delicate, feathery flowers were in such abundance.

The Golden Wattle deserves a place of its own for being our national emblem. Much deservedly so, for its cheery colour is enough to brighten any sad or dull day. It can grow in size from anything to a small ground cover plant to a large tree, mostly with pom-pom flowers.

The Tambo valley is a sight to see at just the correct time. One place in particular, appears before you, the entire hillside painted a bright, shining gold by nature's lush hand. On other hills you would see a spot here and there having dropped from the brush and enlivened the otherwise slightly drab scene. It is a joy to drive that road with each turn displaying its masterpiece.

The Ti-Tree has a small white flower, very insignificant, but with a wonderful bush smell which creates an overall mass of white snow over the bushland. Even now, when I smell it, it takes me back to the Bush.

One other flower which was growing a fair way up the side of a hill on the farm was a very large clump of a type of Easter Daisy with the same delicate, small white flower covering the stems. Mum used to pick very large bunches for the church or fetes, or whatever happened to be on at the time it was in bloom.

PETS

One pet we had was a beautiful snowy-white Persian cat with very long fluffy hair. He was quite friendly when he was younger and there were many photos around with Neil and Prince cuddled together. Prince got a bit cranky as he got older. Old age will do that to some. He would lay in wait in the garden, just at the edge of the path and then jump out, grabbing his unfortunate prey around the ankle, no matter who it may be, even his favourite, digging his claws in and biting.

He got many a smack, but nothing would stop him. I believe he might have quietened down after a while. I think it was the same cat that got caught by Dad on the kitchen table. I don't think there was anything much on the table but just the sight of him on there riled Dad. He grabbed the long toasting fork, the only thing to hand, and swinging it over his head, he brought it down with a great whack and poor Prince went flying. He flew through the air and landed thump! against the cupboards door.

He just lay there for a minute and Dad went to find Mum. "I think I've just killed your cat" he said shakily. Mum gave him an astonished look and ran in to see. Prince was nowhere to be found. "Well, he's not dead" they said and got on with their jobs.

Prince, that evening, strolled nonchalantly in to eat his tea, not showing any signs of hurt, but much, much wiser.

If Prince was in the house thereafter and he heard Dad's step on the path outside, he was off, skidding and sliding, unable to get a grip on the polished floor and finally, with a swish of his long furry tail, he leapt out through the doorway and was gone.

Pity we could not have made him wiser as regards the ambushing trick.

He was never seen on the table again.

Another pet we had was Midge, an Australian Silky Terrier. He came to us as a tiny puppy. He had a black and white body. As he grew, the black hair turned grey from tip to toe. Then eventually the brown hair changed colour too. It was a very pretty effect looking like he had a silver halo all around him. Eventually he became a pretty soft-grey colour all over.

He was a very good tempered pup, always seeming to have a smile on his face and always ready to play with his tail going nineteen to the dozen. His tongue would be lolling to the side of his mouth and his ears would be pricked. The intelligence shone from his eyes. Midge was a very good companion to all of us as he grew; following after each person who he thought needed his company at the time.

BIRDS

We had many different wild birds around our home at the differing seasons. There were the swallows that nested invariably in some area on the house, usually under the eaves. One advantage of their gregarious nature was our ability to quietly creep up and be able to see the baby chicks as and after they hatched.

Most fleetingly were the glimpses of the Robin Redbreast and the Blue Wren. The first glimpse of them ensured that spring was here. There were other myriads of small finches and wrens.

The speed of the Kingfisher skimming across the water after the insects made it difficult to catch much more than a glimpse of it too.

The several varieties of parrot were a joy to see and hear. There was the bright red breast of the King Parrot, the Rosella and the other bright colours of Rainbow Lorikeets and their wonderful, almost bell-like call. The Goldfinches in the Japanese Maple at the side of the house were a delight, as were the Fire-Tails.

The 'Gang Gangs'(the black cockatoos) and white cockatoos were extremely noisy, especially at dusk.

The grey and pink Galahs were very pretty, but they and their cousins, the parrots and cockatoos, often took more than their fair share of the fruit and nuts. The magpies would amuse me at times when the young ones were 'ark-carking' for a worm from their mum. Many times the mum seemed smaller and I would think, "You're big enough to get your own! Leave your poor mum alone!"

They in particular were also a terror for us, as walking, and later riding to school, they would swoop upon us and left bleeding wounds on our heads.

We took to wearing a hat and waving a leafy stick above us. Magpies have been our pets in that they would come for a feed of mince each day and even bring their young with them as they grew older.

My grandmother had a pet magpie named Charlie who was raised from a young fledgling. He would always run around in the garden. I'm not sure, but maybe he couldn't fly. It really had me afraid as a young girl having to go all the way down to the end of the house and around to the back to the toilet. Charlie would wait for me, hiding under the bushes and would dash out and peck my ankles.

I say me, but I guess it chased others too. I would always take a straw broom with me to chase him away. However, the magpie's warble is a wonderful part of the dawn chorus.

There were also the Black Jays, a cousin of the magpie perhaps as it was very similar in looks but with just a touch of white. There was also the Bell Magpie, which may have been the same bird as the Black Jay.

The Willy Wagtails would be a bit of a pest at times. On a summer night, with our windows open, they would be out dancing around on the tap in front of the window and call "sweet pretty creature" incessantly.

I was a really quite flattered at first but it became a problem when trying to get to sleep. They were really quite lovely, black and white in colour, swinging their fanned tails from side to side.

Another bird always looking smart in his black and white plumage was the peewee, a smaller bird than the magpie with more white and a better nature.

There were the kookaburras laughing at our woes and the thrush's distinctive tone. The whip bird with its call sounding like a whip cracking and the plovers' call which raised my nape hair, as I was always told that they were very dangerous as they had a poisonous spur on their heels.

It was so delightful, wandering through the bush hearing the bell birds with their sweet bell tones in song. The lyre birds mimicked all they heard, sometimes, a dog barking, sometimes a whistle to call the dog, and even the sound of an axe. I have almost come to the end of the roll call of birds at our place. The owl, a nocturnal bird was rarely if ever seen but it was a bit eerie at night with its mournful 'Mo-Poke' call.

The crow was not one of our favourites because of its cruelty in pecking the eyes of sheep and lambs whilst still alive and the proud eagle gliding across the sky was similarly not high on our list, taking the whole lambs away.

We realised that it was in order to feed their young, but didn't anyone tell them there were plenty of rabbits and that they were a pest to us?

The 'Chockalar" is named for its repeated raucous cry. Its more common name is the wattle bird. This predator was high on our dislike list for its taking and eating of the young from other birds. It also raided our orchard which did not at all endear him to us.

Starlings nested in the spouting and small openings and their constantly noisy young would drive us mad. They would pull the seedlings out of the vegetable garden and along with blackbirds, scatter the mulch out onto the path.

The swallows would return to build their mud nests on the buildings. One pair would always nest in a corner above the front door, dropping the mud all over the floor of the veranda and down the windows. In the summertime, the swifts would swoop around at dusk, catching the insects and indicating a sign of rain the next day, not causing any trouble.

The ducks, fowl, geese, bantams and turkeys were all part of our farmyard and could not be classed as natives. We had a lorikeet as a pet. It would sit on one's shoulder and was quite tame. Parrots were common to our part of the country and were kept as pets, although we did not have one. My aunt had a cockatoo which was very old. He would talk to you and wander around the garden. The cat and dog treated it with respect.

SWIFT'S CREEK—
THE GENTLE GIANT

The creek always played a big part in our lives. We channelled water from it for the race which, in turn, watered our gardens and animals. Later we pumped water from it using the old Dodge which was also used for wood cutting. We children spent many, many hours during the school holidays swimming and playing in the creek.

Ken and I used to play a game in which we would swim underwater, with our eyes open, towards each other. It seemed like a long way in those days, but looking at the creek these days, there was no place within it that would provide much length for our swimming.

We then progressed with our game and would be required to pick up a number of stones of a certain colour. This would keep us occupied for a long time.

I was thankful for our small skills learned in this game as it really helped later on. I had topped the grade in every subject but one. My arithmetic let me down then. Not a fail, but not as good as my other high marks. However, Mum said to me that if I increased my marks in the next term in that subject, she would give me a treat. Treats were not all that common in those days, so I worked harder than ever. I'm sure you can guess the result of this bribery—I got ninety-nine percent! Mum was very proud of me and, true to her word, after a long journey to Bairnsdale; she presented me with my reward. I was so excited! I couldn't imagine what it could be. "What is it Mum? What is it?" I danced around excitedly. 'You will just have to open it won't you" said Mum with a wry smile. On opening the lovely little box I found my treat. It was a beautiful gold signet ring with my initials and a tiny red stone sparkling at me. I was so pleased with it, jumping around with excitement, thanking Mum and squealing for joy.

"Thank you, thank you, thank you Mummy" I screeched. "I just *lo-o-ve* it. Isn't it beautiful? I will love it forever. Oh I love you Mummy!" I treasured that ring. Really treasured and appreciated that ring

One day, not long after Mum had given it to me, I wore it in swimming. We first had a few dives off the big rock. We wished the rock could be a bit higher so that we could dive deeper. However I'm sure that the rock and the creek would all have to all be a great deal different for this miracle to happen. We ducked, dived and swam, again and again until we were tired.

The cold water shrunk my finger and the beautiful ring dropped off.

I was absolutely distraught, crying and sobbing and in great distress, I joined Ken in our favourite game. This time though it was carried out in utter earnest. I could just imagine how disappointed and cross Mum would be. Besides that was the fact that I adored and cherished that ring. I had worked so hard for it. What was I to do?

We swam and swam and kept looking at the sun to guess how much time we had left before we must go home. I was getting frantic, and so was Ken as he knew how much I loved that ring and how Mum would react. Dad would also be home after finishing the jobs for the day,

At last, with the sun sinking below the surrounding hills, we sadly agreed that we must go home, because to be late would cause further sparks to fly.

We sat there, not wanting to go and getting very upset and tearful again.

We decided to have one more go. We swam back and forth our eyes wide, concentrating on the sight of, or just a glint of, gold.

And then, there it was! I couldn't believe my eyes!! Nestling up against and halfway underneath a small rock. It was just a miracle. We'd found it! We'd found it!

We danced around singing and clutching each other and then raced helter-skelter back home.

I don't know how we contained our excitement as we went inside. Mum said "You're a bit late tonight; you'd better get on with your chores now. Coral, could you please peel these potatoes and Ken, would you bring in some wood please?"

We dashed to get our jobs done with me vowing to myself never, never to go swimming with my ring on in future.

Another story of the creek was when my uncle and his wife and family visited us from Geelong. Uncle Doug loved to go fishing, spear fishing and shooting rabbits at our place. We had all gone down to the creek to cool off and all jumped in and swam and played around. With much ducking and splashing going on until Uncle Doug stood up, pulling on something on his arm. There were several more strange things on him. As he pulled, they just clung on and stretched longer. With him not knowing what they were, or what to do, He yelled "Get them off! Someone get them off!"

They were, of course leeches which people from the city would have no knowledge of. The best way to get them off was to touch them with a hot match or cigarette. Luckily Dad was there to supply the necessary and Uncle Doug was soon rid of them. I don't know until this day why they did not attach themselves to someone else. Needless to say my uncle did not swim in that hole again. For that matter, nor did we.

The creek was a beautiful little stream in the main, but, after heavy rains, would literally roar like a wounded bull. Increasing in size by many, many times it became a great danger. We could see great, huge whole trees, roots and all, being carried off downstream.

It was very frightening seeing its immense power and hearing its distinctive roar.

One of our neighbours' children was drowned one year in the flood. He was only a toddler and when the creek came closer to the houses when in flood, he obviously strayed down into the water and was swept away.

The little footbridge by which we would take a short cut to school, Sunday School and church was washed away. The roads in some places were washed out and large bridges which would take a car were also taken. Many people were cut off from civilisation when this peaceful little kitten roared.

At one stage, after very heavy rain, a new stream came rushing down the gully above the road down the track and straight through into my Auntie's gate. It swept through the gate, which fortunately had been left open, straight down the short drive and through the garage and sheds behind there. It then merrily continued its way to join the creek at the back of the houses. I think it must have had an old map or been given the wrong directions as the water must have gone that way many, many years ago, to have formed that gully.

GOLD PANNING

The creek also, even in my young days, rewarded hard-working men such as Dad and Uncle Clarrie with small gold pebbles washed from further upstream that had settled in the sand and at the side of the water.

I can remember them shovelling sand and gravel into a cradle. The cradle was a long wooden frame, perhaps six foot long, containing metal plates, each plate having smaller holes than the one before.

Then came a layer of blanket—like material stretched along the bottom

Once the sand was shovelled in, the cradle was rocked, hence its name, riddling the sand through the different gauge size of holes. The larger holes separated out the larger, the next size and the smaller until only sand was left in the blanket.

The blanket was then put into the gold pan and all the sand carefully washed out. It was then panned until all you saw was gold shining in the bottom, mixed in with black metallic sand. There were various ways to extract the gold from the sand.

We were taught to pan at a young age but didn't get anything significant. I'm sure Dad and his brother got more from the cradle as a larger area could be treated at the same time.

Later, even when going out with my husband, we would go down to the creek and split the rocks in the middle of the creek.

The rocks were slate-like and would split downwards with a tap from the screw driver prized into the cracks. We would then pan the roots of grass growing in the cracks and the loose partly eroded rock. Our panning process was carried out using a special gold panning dish, made out of tin, with a ridge on one side to hold the smaller particles of gravel and sand and larger pieces of gravel, stones and grass roots. These were swirled about as clean water was taken into the pan as it was inserted side-ways into the water. Dipping the clean water, the pan was then held with the rim away from you, dipping in and rinsing, slowly cleansing away the larger particles with fresh water.

It was good fun but didn't reward us with much of the gleaming golden metal.

Sometimes the gleam of Fool's Gold would lure us on. This was worthless but had fooled many a miner before us.

Another popular pastime provided was fishing. There were not a lot of fish caught in those days, but it was fun trying. Some days enough fish for a meal were caught. Much more rewarding was the spear-fishing. It was probably illegal in those days and I would say that it certainly is now, but it allowed us to put a meal on the table.

The men and boys (Ken remembers this) made their spears from long sticks and some sort of metal shaped into a spear with three or four points. The men would go off with their lantern, sugar bags and spears. They always brought a good number of eels to share amongst us and a few for smoking.

Unfortunately, the little sand trout got in the way of the spear and had to be brought home too. Well you couldn't just leave them there could you? They would make a tasty little morsel for hungry mouths. They were very sweet and it was worth scratching around the bones to get at the succulent flesh. Some of the men and boys perfected the art of 'fish tickling'. After sneaking quietly up to where a fish was resting beneath an overhang the angler very slowly slid his hand under the fish and gently tickled the fish on his belly. Then, very quickly, the fish was flipped out on to the bank. This was an art at which I could never succeed.

Another large part the creek played in our lives was when there was a Bush fire. We were surrounded by fires. The smoke was thick and turned day into night. The embers and bits of burning leaves and bark were blown along by the strong wind. Everyone had to watch to make sure that these did not cause the dry grass around to catch alight. If a strict vigilance was not kept, a new fire could easily be started. We had no vehicle to get us away from there so we headed for the creek.

The creek was not very deep at any place then as it had been a dry summer. We found he deepest hole in the creek, saturated our hessian bags, and crouched down in the water with the wet bags over our heads. As it got darker, we were able to see the fire up along the top of the hills.

I was petrified! What could we do? We just needed to stay wet and use the wet bags to put out any burning embers. We looked up and around us. The fire was creeping down the hills in a 'V' shape as they came down the gullies. It was completely dark now and the fire a bright orange-red. The fire along the top of the hill was a chain of jewels and the burning gullies the droplets of gems. It would have been a good picture, but we were not thinking pictures at this time. We were just fixated on the bright 'V' coming down the hills towards us like a beautiful drop necklace of fire.

The fire was roaring as the gasses in the eucalypts exploded. What a terrifying sound! We were trying not to think what would happen if the fire came right down to us. Was there enough water in the creek to keep us wet? Would our bags stay wet enough to prevent the fire from burning us? How long were we to wait here before the fire got to us? Were we in the best place? Would it burn the houses and all our things?

We crouched and shivered. It was still a hot night but the wind blowing on our wet skin and covering made us cold.

We crouched and shivered, and, almost numb with cold and shock, we looked up. What was happening? Was the wind blowing the fire towards us faster? Something had changed! We all looked at each other and looked to the adults for answers. Wait! Was it really happening? The wind had stopped blowing.

No. The wind was blowing in the other direction! It was blowing the fire away from us! Was it really true? Were we saved?

Then it began to rain.

We had rivers of black water running down our faces. The smoke and soot mixed with—was it the rain or tears? Who cared! We were saved! We laughed and danced around.

After a while, we waited for a time until we were sure that we were really safe and the fire wasn't coming from the other direction.

No it wasn't! The rain had dampened the fire and vegetation down and we were safe to go home. What a relief! We would all need a hot shower and clean clothes when we got home. I'm sure we were all so tired that we would drop off to sleep very quickly.

This traumatic experience left me with a fear of fire for the rest of my life. Even the fire and crackers on bonfire night would be an ordeal for me.

From that time on, in summer when it had been a very hot day and there was smoke in the air and it was windy, I needed to go out several times to ensure there was no bright necklace of fire coming over the hills.

CARS

The old cars were made use of too. I'm sure none of them would have been bought new but we would have got our money's worth. Ken seems to recall the old Dodge, as before mentioned, was used with the saw bench and was the first or one of the first run in Bairnsdale by Dad and his brother. I think this may have been prior to their move to Swift's Creek.

Ken can remember it being down by the creek behind the house. Its main job there was to help pump water up to a tank on a very high stand from which the gardens were then able to be watered by using a hose. This was a really big improvement.

I think this water was also piped to the magical taps in the bathroom and wash house. We had another big, lower tank which collected rain water from the roof. This rainwater was kept for drinking and for use in the kitchen.

The A-model Ford, as I have mentioned, was used for the vegetable run to Cassillis.

The next car I think was the old Cleveland. This car got us to Bairnsdale over that rough and very winding road. Many were carsick travelling that road because of its many bends and steep hills.

There were only heated bricks, wrapped in old rags, to keep our feet warm. The most important things were our umbrellas, not for when we got there, but for the actual journey. I can still remember travelling along with our umbrellas up *in the car!*

The roof leaked so much and the side curtains were made out of some sort of Perspex, which, flapping uselessly, were of little help.

You can imagine the first type of shop that we all rushed into! Anywhere to get a cuppa, as hot as possible, was the order from us all. Maddox Bakery was always our favourite place for lunch too. Their meat pies were delectable, with a flavour all their own. A pie with sauce was all we wanted. It was a real treat for us.

The next was a comparatively modern car the Oldsmobile. It was a good strong, well-built car, which survived my first attempt to drive in it.

It had, for some reason, been parked in the paddock at the top side of the house. The ground was fairly moist and the grass quite slippery.

All went well until I got through the gate. The car slipped sideways into the fence post.

Mum, quite shocked, but amazingly quiet, said "I thought you could drive?" Luckily there was only a small bruise in the bumper bar so all was well.

I had been taking driving lessons with my fiancé, and managed to drive his vehicle without any trouble but the bigger, heavier Oldsmobile was a different matter.

Learning to drive on the winding gravel roads up there gave a good grounding for the future.

The next thing to test out that heavy old warhorse occurred when Mum and we three children were coming home from going to the Pictures in town. It was a big social event which almost the whole town attended each week. Eric Moore used to come from Buchan each week to show the films.

However, on the way home, there must have been frost on the road, because the car slid sideways off the road onto its side. Mum would not have been travelling very fast, and I'm thankful the very large tree had not been that little bit closer. Luckily we were not hurt. Standing on the doors and windows of the other side, we all pushed at the doors above us in an attempt to right the car. Our combined effort was not having much success, so we all breathed a sigh of relief as car lights appeared down the road. The man who helped us out lived a few miles from us up at Cassillis.

The same man, strangely enough, pulled me out of a car accident and took me to hospital, a few years later.

I was so sad to hear many years later that he had died under his overturned tractor. The marks indicated he had tried to drag himself out, before he lost his battle.

I kept thinking, "Why wasn't I there to help him on that day, as he was there to help me on both of those occasions?" I was many miles away at the time. But it makes you think.

The small triangular window at the side front of the car would no longer latch properly as I had put my foot through it. I cannot recall anything else about that night, but he would probably have driven us home and the car was left where it was until the next day.

The next vehicle was a Holden station wagon, which I think kept going for many years later after Dad died.

My Hair

Until I was about twelve years old, I had long blonde sausage-shaped curls to my waist. For special occasions, Mum would put it in rags overnight to help the sausage-shaped curls stay in place the next day.

One day I was playing ball with my older cousin and, of course, he would almost always race me to the ball.

This particular day, I got a paddy up and said "It's this hair! It always gets in the way!" I dashed in to Mum and said "Chop it off. It's just a nuisance."

Mum did not ask me if I was sure, or try to talk me out of it.

She just chopped it off. I dashed in to the mirror and burst into tears. I cried and cried for ages. It looked awful. Mum of course was not a hairdresser, even though she always cut Dad's and the boys' hair and always did a good job.

Perhaps it had become a nuisance to her too, but had never said. She had to help me wash and brush it and perhaps the rags were becoming a chore for her. It was a very real problem with all that hair when I caught nits at school. I sat next to a girl at school who was a real 'Bushie'. I doubt if they ever had a bath or washed their hair. We blamed her for giving me nits. In those days, it was believed that those who got nits were not clean.

Mum and I were devastated. The cure at that time was to wash the hair in pure, undiluted kerosene. After leaving it wrapped in towels overnight, it was combed out next day with a very fine—tooth comb over sheets of newspaper to catch the lice and eggs. It was not a fun, or easy job. This was repeated several times until no more eggs or lice were in evidence.

I was also in bed with mumps at the time. It was not a fun time for me and it was worse for poor Mum.

We had an old couple, Gus and Hilda, living next door to us, in the house where my Aunt and Uncle had lived.

They were both heavy drinkers and were constantly inebriated, morning, noon and night. We would see Hilda, the wife, from our place. In their backyard during the day, she would have a bottle and be lying on the ground, singing to it, or warbling might be a better term.

She would place the bottle a fair way ahead of her and crawl up to it, singing all the time, then have a drink, and repeat the exercise.

We, as children, all thought it was a great joke. Her husband, constantly in the same state, would come stumbling home late at night, singing to himself. At least they seemed to be happy drunks.

Dad and Uncle Clarrie built their house at about the same time as ours, with almost the same floor plan. Now, my bedroom was in the front of the house and I was always afraid that he would come in the front door, turn into the next doorway, thinking it was his own bedroom and come into my room.

I would wake up screaming from this dream. One day, as Mum had not seen or heard Hilda for a few days, she went over next door to check on her. Mum found Hilda with a big gash on her head with maggots crawling around in it. Mum took her to the bush nurse, who had said that Gus must have hit the poor old lady over her head with a bottle. At least she was alive.

Another thing which gave me nightmares was this. Just across the creek, on the track where we would take as a short cut, lived a family who owned a big black greyhound.

I was petrified by it.

One day, when no-one was home, it had come into our yard and snatched my big rag doll, which I had left on the porch. The doll, named Marjie, was nearly as big as me and I loved her to bits. Mum had made her. She was a rag doll, with wool for hair and facial features painted on.

The greyhound had grabbed her and savaged her until she was torn to pieces.

I was really traumatised when I came home and saw it and would have nightmares thereafter that the great big black dog would jump through my bedroom window and get me.

As you have realised from this, we rarely locked our doors, or closed our windows in those days. If we did, it was only when forced to do so by the weather.

Bush Nurse

The Bush Nurse was a lifesaver as the nearest lone doctor was many miles away in Omeo, if there was one available. She would be on call day and night, but was usually to be found at her clinic in town during the day. She was the first person we turned to when an accident occurred or illness struck. She would, along with her colleague in Ensay, have saved the doctor a lot of time and also supported people with their health problems.

In any case, a single lone doctor would not have been able to cover the area from over the mountains at Myrtleford to as far as Bairnsdale.

The Bush Nurse was able to treat minor ailments and had power to prescribe antibiotics and many other medicines which normally a doctor must do. She would attend and give emergency treatment at certain times, such as when a man at the mill chopped some fingers, or even an arm, off.

She was also called out when a woman was in labour and was there for her until she deemed it the correct time for the patient to go to the hospital.

My own Dad at that time didn't have a car. He had to ride on his push-bike for quite a few miles to borrow a car to take Mum to hospital when my brother was born.

Many years on, when I had my first baby, she was also there, and when I had my second and third. As it was a steep and winding road to Omeo, I was afraid I would not reach the hospital in time as my first child had arrived very quickly. She was also responsible for saving my mother's life, for which we will always be grateful.

JACK JUMPERS

When we were at a school sports day at the football ground in Swift's Creek, our family was minus Dad who was at work. We sat collected around a big tree in the shade to have our picnic lunch. Mum was fussing around setting out the scrumptious food she had prepared for us.

Suddenly she gave a squeal. We all whipped around, shocked. It was most unusual for Mum to make such a noise. After all, she was our strong, happy Mum.

However, an ant had bitten her. Not just an ordinary ant, but a Jack Jumper. Almost immediately, Mum's lips started to swell.

Seeing this, one of the dads at a nearby car recognised the danger and bustled her into his car, and sped down to the Bush Nurse.

By the time they reached the clinic, Mum's lips, eyes and face were badly swollen. Wasting no time, the nurse gave Mum an injection and after a while the swelling started to go down. Mum had had an allergic reaction to the bite and could have died very quickly as the swelling could have blocked the airways.

Thereafter Mum was very vigilant about ants, bees and all such stinging, biting insects.

The jack jumper was a black ant with yellow feelers. They jump, with yellow antennas waving around. It would give a nasty bite and swelling at the site to everyone, and the bite would itch for days afterwards. For those allergic to such bites, it could be fatal. I'm glad that no-one else in the family has inherited this tendency.

Some of us have a minor reaction to bites, which swell and itch at the site for a long time, but thankfully, not to the extent of Mum's reaction.

Ken and Neil, both good athletes, brightened the day with at least one red ribbon each for the day.

HYPOL

We would have very few tablets or pills for any ailments in those days, so Mum would try to prevent rather than be forced to cure. I had quite a lot of colds when I was a child and Mum dosed us all with Hypol every night. It is still available now.

It was a more palatable treatment than Cod Liver Oil and Ti-Tree oil which Hypol contained. It is high in Omega 3, Vitamin A and acts as a very good prevention for colds and winter ailments. A nightly spoon of Malt extract was one of our favourite 'medicines'. Malt is the liquid extracted from bran and is said to have all the beneficial ingredients for prevention of cold and flu. So our dear Mum was doing her level best to keep us healthy.

GUY FAWKES NIGHT

Guy Fawkes, or Cracker Night was always a big occasion in our area. We would, for many weeks before, be dragging sticks, branches and anything else which would burn, into a big pile in a tee pee shape. The firecrackers were freely available then, even in our small grocery store. We would choose many different varieties and, combined with those from our cousins, we would have a lot of different types.

We would have the Catherine Wheel which was nailed onto a post, and when lit would turn quickly around, spinning brightly coloured sparks over a large area which would be one of our favourites. The Roman Candle would be set on the ground and would spurt high into the air. The Sky-Rocket was also set into the ground at an angle, pointing up like a rocket. These rockets would shoot high into the sky and could be seen from miles away. They would then burst out coloured sparks to rain down to earth. The Cracker Jacks were a number of small crackers which were joined together and when lit, would jump all over the place, leaving me squealing and hiding behind Mum's skirts. There were many others large and small and everyone would have such fun. Then when the crackers were finished, potatoes would be rolled into the edge of the fire to roast and Damper on sticks would also be cooked to add to our feast. I think we all enjoyed the night even more as the adults would take part in the fun.

I regret to say that I was a party pooper as I was afraid of the crackers and the fire. I have always been afraid of fire. The fire coming over the hills towards us when we were all crouched in the creek, the Cracker Night and when we had to go to Melbourne for a medical appointment and had to drive along the road with fire on both sides.

When I was young and staying with relatives in Geelong, I saw a hugely frightening fire when the wool store was burnt down. It was a gigantic fire and could be seen for miles around. All these incidents added to my great fear of fire.

Mum was very ill when each of her children was born and throughout her other illnesses I cooked the meals, washed the clothes and cleaned for all the family at a very young age. One such time, I had fried some tomatoes to have with sausages and mashed potatoes and I had allowed the tomatoes to burn slightly to the pan.

Dad said then, and always afterwards, that he preferred his tomatoes like that. I was sure that he was just making me feel better, but he always stuck to his guns.

BROWNIES AND GIRL GUIDES

I began going to Brownies when I was the correct age.

I always enjoyed the things we did and were taught. In Brownies and Guides we went for days out in the Bush and were taught how to light a fire with one match, building the fire with only what was at hand in the Bush and not taking anything to help. We would cook Damper and cook eggs in half oranges and potatoes in the fire. A very tasty snack was after removing the cooked Damper from the stick, we would pour golden syrup down into the hole. The Billy was boiled on the fire and the Billy tea was a great thirst quencher

We learnt how to furl and unfurl the flags, both Australian and Group and to respect them both. We were taught how to tie knots, march and many other things which would prepare us for any future occasion.

We would work towards many different badges. Sewing, public service, good deeds, marching, swimming, gardening, tying knots, first aid bandaging and these were just a few. We tried to do a good deed each day. When the required tasks were completed, we would receive our badge.

I loved going for badges and collecting them and we all were so pleased with ourselves as we sewed them onto our uniform.

We were taught to march in formation; marching clockwise whilst the others marched anticlockwise and marching crossing diagonally towards the other group, as well as many other intricate manoeuvres. We would give demonstrations to the public, showing off our prowess.

This marching I greatly enjoyed and would stand up straight and proud in my uniform. I became the flag bearer for the company and it was an honour to march out in front carrying the flag. It was quite heavy and you had to put it into a special holster which was worn around the waist. I washed and ironed my uniform very carefully and polished my brass badges with Brasso and my belt and shoes with shoe polish until they all gleamed.

When you were a pack leader you wore a white cord lanyard to which your whistle was attached. The lanyard had to be soaked and washed and then treated with white shoe cleaner to finish it off. We had to be very careful that we polished the white powder off the lanyard or it would be transferred to our dark brown, and then later blue, of our uniform.

An annual event we practised hard for was marching in the Anzac Day Parade.

We also sang together a lot and I used to sing duets with the company leader who was second in command. I enjoyed this very much and we sang together in a concert.

One big occasion was when we went on a jamboree to Warragul which was attended by all the Guides in Australia. We set up a group next to other Guides and the show ground was packed with companies of Guides with their flag flying proudly.

We were so excited to meet, and exchange badges, with Guides from many different places. We took part in a most joyful program; competing against the other companies in all the things we had been taught. The trip home by train then bus was very quiet as we were all worn out.

It had been a wonderful day, but very tiring in the heat with no shade.

Even now, I believe Scouting and Guiding and all their age-related Groups were and still are now, a wonderful organisation, teaching the young people Bush skills and knowledge suitable for all facets of life. It taught young people self—confidence when promoted to pack leaders, as well as responsibility. I could see this in my son Tony and now in my grandson Nathan. It really is a wonderful organisation and many more young people should become involved, as well as more adults becoming the leaders they are very often looking for.

THE SKY DAY AND NIGHT

One of the things we loved to do in the summer-time as children was to lie on the grass and watch the stars and look for the different constellations. The stars are so bright out there away from towns and light pollution.

Another of our favourite things was to lie and watch the clouds and make castles and trees and animals in the clouds and be mesmerized as the clouds moved and formed other shapes.

BIRTHDAY PARTIES

When I was young we all had very large birthday parties but only on special birthdays, not for every one.

There were so many children living in and around the scattered homes in our valley. There were the Miles children who were four in one family, the Goldie's, the Frasers, Robert Mayne who lived in the wattle daub cottage and my three cousins next door, plus we three children. In the photos in Mum's collection there showed probably fifteen or more attending. After I started school, there would be school friends as well.

We all had mountains of cakes, biscuits, sausage rolls and fairy bread. For those who don't know, fairy bread was slices of bread spread with butter then sprinkled with hundreds and thousands. There was always the special birthday cake with candles for the number of years old we were. All these goodies were home made by the mothers, often helped by the girl or girls in the family.

In our family there was always a special plum pudding to celebrate our birthdays. There were always silver coins hidden in the pudding and no one knew who would get one or more or none. This was not served at the party but at the family meal. We were unable to use the decimal coins as they were not silver.

For quite a while after decimal coins came in, Mum would swap the threepences and sixpences for decimal coins and put the silver ones away for the next birthday plum pudding. This traditional plum pudding with silver coins in it was usually a Christmas treat, but my family, from my Mum's side always had one at birthdays as well. I'm not sure if anyone else followed this custom for birthdays.

We all played children's party games with balloons and party hats and had a wonderful time. It would be fairly unusual for a modern family to have so many guests as it is now so expensive and all the guests must be given take home treats. It was our custom to send a piece of cake home with each child, wrapped in a serviette.

We had quite a few dress-up social outings whether it was for birthday parties or school or Sunday school, I'm not sure. I can just remember a cat outfit Mum made for me. I hope the photo is still around. Mum went to a lot of trouble with it. I was completely covered head to toe in a black suit, complete with tail and long white whiskers. I believe I won a prize for that outfit.

DOG PHOBIA

When I was about thirteen or fourteen years old, my friends and I were sitting at our desks together during lunch time.

We were chatting and giggling as teenager girls tend to do. My very best friend was laughing so hard that she started to cough. She coughed and coughed until suddenly, she was coughing up blood. We were all badly in shock but someone ran for a teacher.

The ambulance came and took her to hospital. We were all concerned about her and couldn't wait to find out how she was. Eventually it filtered down to us that she had had an operation and was alright.

Rene has had no lasting effect from this problem except for a large scar on her side. I will always remember that event and I now have a phobia about touching dogs, because Rene had a large hydatid cyst removed.

Hydatid disease is caused by tapeworms picked up from patting dogs, in particular farm dogs, which have been fed raw meat in which the eggs or worms have been living. This can be passed on to humans when they touch a dog and don't wash their hands.

Since then I have been paranoid about touching animals without washing my hands. I love animals, but from afar. No matter how much I love an animal I will rarely touch, pick them up or cuddle them.

If I do, I am very uncomfortable until I have washed my hands. It is amazing how a traumatic incident can effect one for many, many years to come.

TEASING

I was teased for many years at school by older girls, some of whom later became good friends. I was school captain and had dimples. So one name I was called was 'Captain Dimply-Dimps'.

Another was 'Polyps' because they said that coral was just made up of dead polyps.

Almost all was because of jealousy as I was always top of the class and was quite popular with the teachers. On complaining to the teacher, he said that I should be flattered and take it as a compliment. This did not help.

I was always quiet and shy and very easy-going and slow to anger. However, push me too hard, and the fur would fly, sometimes literally. One girl at school found this out, both to her regret and mine, as the chunks of hair pulled out from my head were nearly as bad as hers.

One day a teacher made the comment, "Any resemblance between you and an angel is purely accidental."

First Day

I had started school a bit later because of the polio scare at that time. At least one child died from the disease and many more were very sick.

One boy actually died at school. He had crawled around the back of old chalk boards, trestles and other junk in a shelter shed. It took ages for them to get him out.

A boy who became my husband and eventually my ex contracted the illness at that time but was lucky to get away with a light dose. He was left with one leg quite a bit shorter than the other.

One girl named Glen who had a bad, but not fatal dose was actually to become my sister-in-law. For quite some time afterwards, when she had recovered from the worst and infectious stage, she was brought to school on a bed with wheels on it. Made from timber, it was something we had never seen before. She was propped up with pillows but was unable to walk. She was, and is, a pretty girl, very brave and determined and also quite intelligent.

Eventually she was able to walk with irons on both legs and two sticks. As time went by Glen became very independent, driving a specially modified car and she worked at one stage at the manual telephone exchange.

One leg improved somewhat but one remained paralysed. Glen married and had two children and went on to top jobs in Telstra in Melbourne. One job required her to be jumping on and off air planes and flying around Australia.

In the meantime she was having a sad life, tragically losing many members of her family, including a son, and her marriage. I admire and love her very much. I don't know how she managed it all. Plenty of intestinal fortitude I'm sure.

My First Day at School

It was my first day at school I had to walk the three miles on my own.

Come lunch time, I was off. Bawling all the way, I was finally found at the top of Charlie's Cutting; a very steep hill on the road home.

Subsequent trips were made accompanied by my older cousin Jim, and later my brother Ken and then June and Rhonda.

Neil was a fair bit later and I think we were able to catch the school bus about half way along by the time he was going to school. I rode to school from part-way there on the handlebars of a boy who worked in the local grocery store. Then I would get a ride home in a truck driven by a man delivering things to the farms. It seems that I only got rides one way at these times. I must have walked back the other way.

At another time, we were getting rides with a teacher who lived at Cassillis and drove past our place each day. That did not last for long as she decided she was not prepared to take the risk of being sued if she had an accident with us in the car.

I seem to remember a time when we caught the Eastern Road lines bus. The driver lived in Cassillis and for a time would drive past our place each morning at the correct time for us. He made this trip from Omeo and Bairnsdale and back, taking passengers, mail and parcels each day. We were often running late catching this bus, scrambling up the steep track carrying schoolbags and all, and catching it by the skin of our teeth.

Later we got bikes and rode them to school. The frosty mornings our fingers would freeze and my legs got white blotches from the cold (as I only wore a uniform skirt) and turned red when they warmed up.

I can only remember wearing slacks once in those years. It was on a school trip to the snow and they were a pair of light coloured, wool mix slacks.

I believed I looked hideous in them. I saw a photo of myself wearing the slacks and it persuaded me to stick to dresses or skirts. In the photo I was sitting on a log and, in that position, my thighs looked huge.

It was around that time, only in summer, I was wearing a pair of shorts around the house. Mrs Hilda was comparatively sober and said. "Look at those thighs; they are as big as a leg of ham." With me being a sensitive and self-conscious person, I took it to heart and did not wear slacks at all until after I was married. I was quite slim at that time and would love to be as slim now. I believe that was the beginning of a very long and frustrating battle with my weight.

In the spring the magpies swooped at us on two different places along the road. At one stage Jim was pecked on the head by one, making it bleed. We soon learnt to wear hats and wave leafy sticks above us to deter them. I of course would be howling in fear.

SCHOOL BUS

Even when it was deemed that we may catch the school bus partway down the road, we would still have to ride past those places where the magpies swooped.

One day after riding from home to catch the school bus, I was as usual, running late. I was careering down the steep, long hill just before the bus stop and the chain slipped off my bike. Up I went, over the handlebars and landed with a splat on the hard road!

The bus driver saw me and came back to help me. I was not hurt much and just had skinned knees and a few bruises. I was able to continue to school for the day. That bus driver would never wait for us if we were running late. He would be able to see us as we came around the bend at the top of the hill. If it was the exact time when he was deemed to be leaving that stop, he would be off. I don't know how many times I stood, gasping and panting, staring hopelessly at that yellow bus racing away from us.

At times, not often enough, we would take the short cut across the creek walking to Sunday School and Church at 'The Walnuts'.

Sometimes the foot bridge would be washed away by flood waters. We would cross over a two and a half feet wide rail less, swaying bridge.

We would then walk along a flat track and up around the side of the hill parallel to, but quite a way from, the rivers bend, then down to meet the creek and cross over a more sturdy bridge capable of carrying vehicles. This saved us quite a few miles.

THE WALNUTS CHURCH

'The Walnuts' was where the Methodist church was in those days. The name was taken from the line of huge walnut trees in front and to the side of the church. Those walnut trees were actually planted by Dad's grandfather many, many years ago. Beneath the walnut trees was the site of a butchers shop owned by the Bouchers years ago when the trees were young or just planted. Directly in front of the church was a thick, high cypress hedge. We would often play in the hedge and, for some reason, would find it great fun. I'm sure it was full of dust and that we would be covered in it.

It was quite a sight with the line of all the women folk and the children taking the shortcut to church. The line strung out like mother duck and her ducklings with Mum and Auntie Con, Jim, June and Rhonda, Ken and myself with Grandma Barnes striding out pushing the pram with Neil in it. Grandma Barnes, Mum and Aunties Co. were resplendent in their fox stoles. The fox was draped over the shoulders and was biting its brush to keep it in place.

No one could get Dad or Uncle Clarrie to church.

We children would first go to Sunday school and would need to learn passages from the Bible and would often be rewarded with a bookmark with a biblical verse and picture on it. We were proud of ourselves when we were able to take this home to show Dad.

At the end of the year or some annual event we were given prizes for regular attendance and for learning the texts and other tasks.

We were all given a book at some stage and I, for one, valued that book and treated it with care and added it to my growing collection. I always treated books with respect and if I saw anyone turning a page down I thought was vandalism.

The church was a real social affair. We had tennis matches, just a bit further down the road, where we all worked to keep the court playable. I recall many Saturdays just before the season, spending many hours, along with quite a few others hoeing grass off the court, raking it and marking the lines to get the court ready for our first match.

TENNIS AT THE WALNUTS

Mum and Dad, Ken and I all played with a lot of others each Saturday. I recall Neil being in the pusher and all of us taking turns to care for him and the other little ones. At the beginning of the season, we would all take part in a working Bee, or even several.

Then when all was ship-shape, we would begin to play tennis. Everyone had a hit and it was an enjoyable afternoon. Every now and then, someone would pop one over the high fence or through a hole the cattle had made in it. Some of us young ones would be rostered to race around and return the ball to the players, sending the cattle racing off in alarm. A lot of good—natured slanging came from the gallery at times, and very much laughter.

I can remember sitting in the shade of a tin shed to have our afternoon tea. We all took our own drinks and food and would share it around. I don't know when I stopped playing tennis there. Maybe it was when I started work.

I remember trying to play a good few years later, after having my children. I was a complete flop. I don't know if I had forgotten I had once played tennis and could have a respectable match with someone, or the skill just fades after that many years without practice.

Unfortunately my back also objected to that particular exercise.

SOCIAL NIGHTS

We often had social nights at the church and a night called 'Salamagundi' which meant 'all sorts'. Different types of games would be played that night. Ken can remember playing 'Bobs', which was played by placing a board on the floor with arches cut into it and sides opening out to form a guide so that balls would be kept to the playing area. The arches had numbers painted above them and balls shot towards the arches with a cue stick would score an amount for each arch. I have not seen or heard of it since.

Another game we played was 'Poor Pussy'. The players all sat around in a circle and one person was chosen to be the cat. The aim was for the cat to make the chosen person laugh. The cat would rub his face up and down the legs making an elongated *'Meo-o-o-w'* noise. The chosen person was to keep patting the cat, saying poor pussy and trying their best not to laugh, which they were certain to do eventually. There was no 'if' with regard to the laughing because the increasing length of the meows and crazy actions by the cat made it impossible! Of course all the others in the room would be laughing their heads off. This did not help at all! However when the person being picked on laughed, he or she would become the cat. The game then continued until all players had had a turn at being the cat. Very rarely someone was able to remain poker faced and he/she would win the game.

Another game that caused great glee was 'Pass The Balloon'. This, I would think, is a more well-known game. To explain in more detail: the balloons were blown up as high as possible, partners allocated, and the game began. The balloon was placed under the chin of the first player then he/she with hands always behind the back endeavoured to pass the balloon to the partner. This person would then pass the balloon to the next. This sounds easier than it was as the balloons got into strange places and you can imagine a man with the balloon at his waist trying to pass the balloon to the next woman's chin. The mind boggles. All these antics again created a great deal of laughter from the participants and the onlookers.

Another equally laughter-generating game was trying to walk the length of the room with the balloon tucked between the knees.

'Spin The Bottle' was another more well-known game that we enjoyed. A large number of such games were played and a dance was also put on to complete the program. These nights were always well attended and everyone joined in the games.

Another social night would be held with only dances on the program.

Another was community singing and many more such nights brightened our lives. Mum was a beautiful singer and was often asked to sing in church and for weddings.

As I got older I was also asked to sing. I remember one day, after the church building was moved to the town, a special service was held to commemorate the opening of this church in its new position. Many people, who had attended church in the original place and previous ministers and other special guests, came back. I was asked to sing at this service. I was roughly sixteen years old and was very, very nervous. If I recall correctly I sang 'I'll walk with God' and was very well received and congratulated from all directions. I was very flattered and pleased that I could add to the joy of the day.

Mum's flowers were, of course, beautifully arranged to add to the scene. I often helped Mum with the arranging of the flowers every week in the church. She however had a magic touch and was able to place the arrangement into a much better order than I could.

No matter what the season, Mum would always have something from flowers and even foliage, to arrange each week. Even in the winter and autumn, the gloriously different coloured leaves would brighten a dull corner. In the correct season we often picked the gum tips in their entire colourful array.

YOUNG CRUSH

One particular minister was relatively young and I had quite a crush on him.

I always dressed as well as I could for church but I tried even harder to be sophisticated. I think this was after I started work, but still did not have a lot of money, and I believed in saving as much as possible. I had a green suit, a rather dull green, but I would brighten it up with hats, gloves, shirts underneath or scarves. The suit had a slim skirt and a little peplum to the jacket.

I used to make my hats at that time, making them from bases made out of a stiffened material in many different shapes. These I bought at Foards in Bairnsdale. I would cover the bases with a lemon material and add an artificial flower or two, some sequins and a bit of netting. To make the outfit I would wear a little lemon jumper underneath and lemon gloves. I made a red hat and did the same with the other accessories and I think I had another colour to ring in the changes. I made most of my own clothes at that time and I would be looking forward to our monthly trip to Bairnsdale to buy material, cotton, buttons, zips and patterns and whatever else was needed.

Darning the socks, jumpers and linen was also a time consuming, and never-ending job, as was patching trousers and shirts. Mum and I spent many hours at this task. I was not very good at this job as it was difficult to get the darn to look like a piece of woven material with the wool or cotton filling in the hole, using a wooden mushroom under the darn. A very useful tool still used by a few today, looking exactly the same.

A very unkind remark was often made about having to pass items down to siblings which we had clothes made out of. Most of the time we used the old Singer treadle sewing machine and were thrilled when we were able to buy an electric version. This was not until after I was married as I can remember sewing clothes for my children.

We made these periodic trips to the nearest large town to stock up on groceries, clothes and all the things not available at our local store. We would buy sugar and flour in hessian bags. These bags were then made use of in many ways once they were empty and washed out

BATS IN THE STORES

In Bairnsdale at the big department store I was fascinated by the method of conveying change from the central office back to the counter. Wires were strung willy-nilly around and across the ceiling of the store, as far as my childhood memory recalls.

Each counter lady would have a small jar or tin with a lid on it. Into this she would place the money paid by the customer, and the invoice for the sale. Putting the lid back, on she would screw the tin into the overhead receptacle. After the salesperson's ringing of the bell, they flew like bats back to the office. The person or persons in the office would extract the money and paperwork and, after inserting the change and receipt, would then, via the bat-line, return this to the counter. It was then given to the customer. It was fascinating and noisy to my country eyes and ears. Like bats they flitted across the ceiling, bells ringing, wires whirring and these little black things swooping around.

I was, of course, afraid of bats as I imagined them being caught in my hair, and my hair having to be cut to get it out. I squealed and hid my head when any came near.

RED PETTICOATS

At around this time a group of teenagers came from a youth group in Melbourne. They were billeted around the church families and arrangements had been made to amuse them over the few days they were there.

Two of them were billeted at our place and two and my friend Margaret's place. More of the visitors were billeted at other homes.

Margaret lived with her Grandmother in a charming old house just up their lane from the church. I had always been fascinated by that house for some reason. With rooms off verandas here and there it also had a beautiful big walk in pantry which I'm sure was large enough for one could cook a meal in. Well perhaps not cook, but prepare, as the stove and oven were in the kitchen.

They kept hens in a very large area which was nearly as big as a cow paddock.

I sometimes stayed there overnight and was always put in the big bed which I thought was Grandma Miles'. The bed had knobs on the bedposts which could be screwed off. I suppose the house was vaguely antique looking. Perhaps that explained my fascination.

I and the girl who was billeted with us were at Margaret's to get ready for some social event or dance at the church. The Melbourne girls had red Petticoats. I did not know what the significance was, but to me it seemed a bit racy. The newcomers were all a bit strange to us. I guess they felt the same about us. We showed them how to trap, kill and skin a rabbit and of course how to cook it.

I'm not sure how all of this went down but we didn't have anyone faint on us. The boy who was staying with us had a bad cold. He wandered around all day with tissues stuck up his nose. Why would that stick in my memory?

BLACKBERRIES

At the correct time of the year, a pleasant chore was to go black-berrying. As the berries grew bigger and sweeter close to the water, off we went in our gumboots, hats and gloves. Wading up the creek, we would pick and pick and pick! We kept a sharp eye out for snakes, as they would be heading towards water in the heat of the day.

For some reason it took a long time to fill our buckets at first. Do you think that the system being one for the bucket and two for the mouth was part of the problem? However, as we started to get quite full, the buckets started to fill more quickly.

Quite often, we all piled into a car and went further up towards Cassillis for the berries. They were a bit later in that location and we would be able to pick them there when our own area was picked out. The blackberries are well-known as a fruit to most people now, likely because of their more recent availability in the shops. They were a great delicacy so large and sweet and only available in the Bush areas.

These tasty little morsels were best in a bowl with a generous helping of cream or ice cream. We ate a few like this but most went into bottles, so that we could enjoy them all year round. We would pick enough for preserving and then many went into jam.

Blackberry jam was a real favourite. Many different varieties of jam was made, some of them were: plum, plum and raspberry, quince jelly, apple jelly, and grape jelly, marmalade, cherry plum jelly and fig jam and gooseberry jam, marmalade and a very popular one was carrot and lemon marmalade Another less known was greengage plum jam.

Some of the marmalades were not very popular with the younger children, but all the others went into school lunches. Melon and lemon, nectarine, apricot and melon and pineapple just about completes the full list of jams, all made by Mum and I. We always made enough to put on stalls at fairs or street markets.

We really enjoyed this chore, 'slaving over a hot stove', as it was usually in Summer when the fruit was ready to picked and processed. It was a crime to see fruit wasted.

Even in her eighties, Mum would be out tying old dresses and shirts to the branches of the trees in her smaller back yard to try to keep the birds away. Mum would freeze the fruit, even though her freezer was almost full with fruit frozen from the year before. She would take fresh fruit and jam to 'club'. She would also make bottles of jam, which she was unable to eat because of her diabetes.

No-one wanted to pay very much, and Mum said she was selling it for less than the price of the sugar. She would worry about fruit on the neighbours' trees being wasted.

The black-berry, unfortunately, was declared a noxious weed and like all other noxious weeds, farmers were required to eradicate them from their farms. The crown land areas, like the roadsides and the creek banks were all sprayed by men employed by the Department of Lands. This was a great shame, but they in a similar way to other introduced species, became a pest and would take over good grazing land.

This practice of spraying by the Lands Dept., in years to come, kept the food on the table for my children and us, as my then husband was employed in this way for many years.

AN EXCITING STEP FORWARD

At last! The great day was here. We were all so, so excited!

Can you imagine what a gigantic change it could be? We had been on tenterhooks with the passing of each day, the question being, "Is it today? Is it today?" from each of our mouths.

Things had been *slo-o-o-wly* progressing, with holes being cut into walls, wire all around and those funny glass things. What was it?

"Well come on" you say, "don't keep us in the dark any longer." Well of course you've guessed by now.

The Power! Electricity! No more candles! But Mum said we had to keep some candles for emergencies. In the shed which Dad had built on to the back of the wash house, there was a bank of batteries. There might have been about eight or ten, all coupled together, and in an adjoining room, a motor.

Switches were thrown and there was light, just like at Grandma's house in Geelong.

For quite a while we basked in the pleasure of not having to clean and fill all the lamps each night and not have to carry one, or light another, each time we moved from room to room.

Gradually new gadgets would appear as we were able to afford them. I'm not sure which came first, but when we had a 32 volt iron, the engine needed to be started as there was not enough power in the batteries to run such a thing.

We gradually obtained most of the appliances. The refrigerator was the first big appliance we afforded as it was important to keep the food fresh.

Then eventually came the washing machine. What a back saver! What a time saver! How easy to do the washing!

At first the machine did not have a mangle, which was a huge improvement on all the wringing by hand. Then as time went by and a new washing machine was needed, we progressed to the next model.

It had a mangle which was mounted between the two wash troughs. We would put the clothes into the machine, between two rollers. They were then wound through by hand.

Once again the engine must be started to have enough power to do the washing. Gradually, new appliances and gadgets were added.

We had a 32 volt record player, radio, even a 32 volt Mixmaster and sewing machine. Weren't we becoming indolent with all these machines to help us with our work?

TELEVISION

I don't believe we had any television until after the 240 volt electricity came along.

When we were eventually able to receive television it was from a signal receiver or transmitter on the top of Flagstaff Hill, just outside the town of Swift's Creek, run by local men. We were, at first, only able to receive ABC channel and of course it was all in black and white. It was just magic to have pictures come to us in our homes. As we knew no better, we revelled in the one channel we could get at the time.

MILKING

We milked our three or four cows by hand. We began by putting their head in the bail, so they couldn't get away. If the cow was known to kick, we would leg-rope her. i.e. tying a rope around her nearest leg so she could not kick.

A kick could result in the bucket of milk being kicked over and thus wasting it and a kick from a cow would certainly make you sit up and take notice and leave a respectable bruise.

One day I remember. I was sitting on my milking stool, busily tugging away, the milk with its distinctive sound, rhythmically singing into the slowly and filling the pail, when, suddenly, splat! I was on the ground on my back, covered in milk, my legs high on the cow's side and Daisy letting out a triumphant, "Mooo!"

What a mess. Maybe I was not properly awake that morning as either I had not recognized Daisy the kicker or just forgotten to leg-rope her. Some of the cows, all being called by name, were very quiet and would stand quietly whilst they were being milked. Others would take great delight in smacking you on the leg or the nearest part of your anatomy with that great big foot, if you weren't careful.

I was not popular that morning because of the wasted milk. Something I felt quite badly done by for, feeling it unfair to be blamed for an accident. However I *had* been careless not to recognize the cow and leg-rope her.

The milk, on making it safely home, was put through a machine called a separator. This was a complicated thing with many stainless steel cones nestled into each other and other complicated paraphernalia. It was a real pain to clean. This machine was once more operated by turning the handle as quickly as possible This separated the cream from the milk. This chore was another of those that was simplified later on by modernization, once the electricity came to our sleepy valley.

This was a comparatively modern machine, because before its advent, the milk was let to stand in a cool place for a day or so. This allowed the cream to rise to the top to be skimmed off.

Another way to separate the cream from the milk was to heat it to boiling point. This had the advantage of the milk having a longer shelf life. The cream also rose to the top and was skimmed off. This changed the flavour of both products, not popular with some. I for one really loved scalded cream on my bread and jam. Scalded cream was not suitable for making butter.

MAKING BUTTER

Making butter was a necessary chore to those of us who had cows and who lived as much as possible from the products of our land.

We were able to sell it to friends who did not have cows and who preferred the creamy taste of the hand churned butter to the more processed dairy fare. I remember making about two pounds of butter at a time. It would depend on the amount of cream we had to use on the day. The cream was left to sour and become quite thick and was then put into a butter churn. The butter churn was made of wood and was a square box with rounded bottom and a lid. A handle on the side, was attached to a bar going through to a set of paddles inside. These paddles mixed the cream, doing the job of our modern day food mixers. On went the lid and away we went, turning and turning and turning until our arms felt like they were dropping off.

We would then swap arms and churn some more. With a bit of luck someone would come in to take over. They would be dragged, kicking and screaming out their protests to no avail, because the butter must be churned and we needed a rest. He or she was generously given a turn at churning until their arms got tired.

It's amazing though, that our muscles became used to the exercise and we could churn for longer and longer without a break. After a bit of a rest, we continued until you could tell by the sound, and the feel, that the cream was, turning to butter at last. We added a small amount of salt and the swishing noise meant that the liquid had been extracted from the cream.

On tipping off the buttermilk, we divided the butter into smaller pieces and using wooden butter pats, one in each hand, we would squeeze the last of the liquid out.

We then took time patting it and shaping it, at first on the side where the pats had the diamond shaped grooves, and then on the smooth side. It was essential to get all the liquid out, and the grooves helped in this, otherwise the butter would not last as long. Once the liquid was all out, we used the smooth side to shape it neatly into a rectangle. Much like the half pound of butter one sees today.

Working on the remaining pieces, we finished the job by wrapping each portion in greaseproof paper and then put them into the Coolgardie safe or fridge, depending on the level of cooling needed.

BUTTER CHURNS

There were several different types of churn during that time that we used. Some were like a wooden drum standing on end with the churning being done by pushing a handle up and down. Some were even made out of glass.

Butter is churned today, if anyone wants to do it, with a modern Mixmaster. A much easier task.

A Butter Factory was opened in 1907 to which the local farmers took their cream to be made into butter. At its peak it manufactured 55 tons of butter, but, because of unreliable weather in that area, it was forced to close in 1946. I remember going to collect butter or cheese from that building after the factory had closed. These products were brought from the nearest factory and were sold back to the farmers in payment, or part payment, for cream provided. This must have been when we were too busy to churn butter.

I did take up buttermaking again after I was married when cash was short.

The Local Store

The local store carried many things from shovels to candles, liquorice to liniment, ice cream to soap. Biscuits were stored in large square tins, with a tin for each type. Many tins sported the now famous colourful parrot. If one wanted a mixture, the shop keeper would put some of each into a brown paper bag.

One could, if short of money that week, buy a bag of broken biscuits at a reduced price. It seemed that no matter how much care was taken with the tins; there were always broken ones in the bottom.

Flour was scooped out of a big tin container and weighed carefully on the scales.

Sugar, tea, and other perishables were bought by the pound and put into brown paper bags.

The scales were large, and made out of copper. They had a flat plate on one side and on the other side, a bowl shaped container to put the foodstuffs in. Potatoes, carrots, pumpkin, dried fruit, everything would pass over those scales.

On the flat tray was placed a weight ranging in size from a half ounce, going up through the ounces to the one pound I think, or maybe it was even two or five pounds?

All things had to be weighed even to the lump of cheese cut off a large two pound wheel or slab. Dad was very fond of cheese and he liked it very tasty. He called it rat's cheese. I have inherited the Boucher taste in this regard. Mum would bring home a large piece, which would last Dad all week in his sandwiches

Dad invariably liked jam and cheese sandwiches with no variety at all. That's just all he wanted, with a slight variation in the flavour of the jam. Apricot jam and cheese was his favourite. I must say I agree with him.

As time went by and we had a more reliable car, we would take a monthly trip to Bairnsdale and buy our flour and sugar in bulk, again in those so useful flour and sugar bags.

As children, we always looked forward to shopping day, as Mum would come home with a bag of mixed lollies which was diligently divided between the three of us.

There was a fair amount of swapping going on as one preferred a particular type to the other. It was strange how these lollies were consumed, with me eating mine fairly quickly, Neil even quicker and then to Ken, who always made his, in some magic way, last until the next ration.

Ken was always very particular and his toys would be cared for so well that they looked almost new some years hence. Neil always seemed to pull his apart to see how they worked, even in his teens. Some did get put back correctly, but some did not. Woe betide if he was caught playing with Ken's toys. They shared a bedroom and Ken's side was always neat, and Neil's not so neat. Ken would strongly object if some of Neil's things strayed onto his side.

When I later had a little bit of money to buy some myself, I would go for liquorice blocks. These lasted a long time and were something like twelve for a penny or some unthinkable price and would keep me going for ages.

On shopping day Mum almost always came home with about six of the local baker's meat pies. We regarded this as a treat and looked forward to Saturday for those lovely meaty pies.

The bakery at Swift's Creek had an ancient wood burning oven, which, many still say, makes the best bread.

In any case the bread was very good whether because of the baker or the oven. People would come from other towns in the area for that bread and those pies. The football club often had pie nights, so the baker would be extra busy then.

SCALES

Speaking of those scales, the post office had a very similar set, but much, much smaller. These were used to weigh the letters and parcels.

When I worked in that Post Office many years after, when my children were little, those tiny scales still did the job.

The butcher shop also had a set for weighing the meat. The ladies of the house went into the butcher shop for their weekly meat ration. The meat was always cut exactly as requested. It was then wrapped in butcher paper and finished with several sheets of newspaper. The whole parcel was then tied with string into a neat parcel. The string was tied in a knot and a loop added to allow the parcel to be carried easily.

The string was then broken off by those amazingly strong fingers. How many have tried to emulate this trick, to their sorrow. Perhaps it was the technique learned only by butchers. Perhaps his fingers had been toughened by many years of this practice. Periodically an official from the weights and measures department would come and check all the scales in the town to make sure they weighed correctly, and adjusted them when needed.

RABBITS

Rabbits were one animal which was in plague proportions in those days and farmers could be fined if they did not try to eradicate them from their land.

The rabbits introduced into this country were so well suited to the Australian climate they became too prolific. They were eating the feed meant for the sheep and cattle from which the farmers were attempting to make a living. In their native country, the rabbits did not become such a problem because the climate with the snow bound winters slowed down their multiplication.

The head per acre was so much lower when their numbers were so high. Once the rabbits were cleared out the head per acre for a property increased dramatically.

The methods used to eradicate the rabbits may sound cruel to the dear little bunnies, but in many cases it was, literally, a choice between the food for the farmers' children or the bunnies. Many different methods were used to try to keep them under control. One was to use ferrets.

These were long, slim animals with a vicious bite. These ferrets were sent into the burrows to frighten the rabbits out of another exit in the warren where someone would be waiting to dispatch them. One of the problems with ferrets would be their tendency to stay in the burrows or come out of a hole a lot further away. The farmer was then without his ferret.

The next method was the rabbit trap—a cruel method and banned in the present times. The traps were usually set at the mouth of burrows attached to a peg by a strong chain. A shallow hole was scraped out with the setter which was designed especially for this job. It was wide and fairly blunt at one end and was hammer-like at the other end.

This was used to hammer in the pegs. The trap jaws were pressed open and held with one hand with one finger gingerly holding the plate up so that the trap did not go off and catch a finger. This however was not an unusual occurrence. A trap paper, previously cut out of newspaper, was placed over the plate so that the dirt did not fall under the plate when it was sprinkled over it. Special care was taken to cover the trap and chain so the rabbit could not see them.

Quite a few traps were set each evening, depending on the number of traps to hand and the time available to set them. Sometimes you might have a dozen to twenty set each night. The next morning we would go around the traps and collect any rabbits caught.

After wringing their necks they were put into a sugar bag to take them home. When I first started setting traps I was unable to wring their necks. I didn't have the strength in my hands and wrists. I tried other things to knock them out, which may sound a bit cruel here, so I won't elaborate.

I would take the live rabbit's home for an adult to dispatch them. On occasion, one or two would escape if I had not stood on the end of the bag properly. Something I got cross about as I then thought, "All that work for nothing".

Oh well, I would console myself that I would probably catch them again another day. I would take them home and then prepare the carcass for sale or for the table.

Not only did they provide us with much needed meat for the table during the depression, but feed for the animals too. We were also able to sell the skins, after being stretched and dried on special wires, to men who dealt in the rabbit fur trade. This gave a few more shillings in the coffer.

The 'Rabbit-O' would come around periodically to collect them and add some more pence to an often light purse. The cleaning and skinning of the rabbits was often a long chore after the trap rounds.

The whole thing was repeated the next day. The rabbits also became food for the dogs and cats on the farm and at one stage I was selling fresh, skinned rabbits to shops in town. We were also able to provide the meat to other families around who did not have the necessary equipment.

Young rabbit done in egg and breadcrumbs was very tasty and not unlike chicken.

Rabbit stew was another tasty dish.

Another method was to shoot them. Men went out at night in vehicles with spotlights. They not only shot the rabbits but foxes too which were also a serious pest.

Another method of eradication in this never ending war was to dig out the burrows. This was a lot of hard work and not too successful as the warrens would go underground for a long way.

The dogs liked to helps in these methods.

Fumigation was another quite successful way. The burrows would be blocked at one end and a poisonous bomb was lit, thrown into the burrow, and then the holes filled in. The problem with this was the burrows often had multiple exits and entrances and you would see a cloud of smoke coming out of a hole quite a few yards away.

One more method employed in this long battle was the poisoned trail. Fortunately the Department of Lands and Survey in those days provided the fumigants and the poison for the trail. A trail was scraped with a one blade plough pulled behind the horse. This trail was scraped around the contours of the dry, rocky hills. Carrots were then usually used (supplied by the Lands Department) to give a free feed. We would just chop up carrots and dribble them along the trail.

After one or two days of giving the rabbits a free feed, the farmer could see where the most carrots had been taken from and was able to ration out the poisoned carrots in the most heavily populated areas.

After the poison had been put down, early the next day, the dead rabbits were picked up and buried so that the sheep, cattle and farm dogs did not eat the poisoned rabbits. Of course all the stock needed to be shifted out of the paddock before being baited.

THE RABBIT DRIVE

One fun day was set up before the poisoning and everyone took part in the Rabbit Drive.

The drive took part in one of our paddocks on the other side of the hill. The fences came to a meet in a triangle up at the top of the hill and a piece of wire netting was put ready to close off the bottom of the triangle when the rabbits were in.

Everyone; adults, children, friends, neighbours and dogs of all shapes and sizes, all joined in. They used tins filled with stones, hooters, bells, pots and pans whacked with spoons, whistles and toots, anything that made a noise, heading off for the top of the hill.

The boys thought this was great as they could try out their best war cries without being told to "Be quiet!"

We climbed and scrambled the steep and rough terrain, clambering over rocks, big and huge, under and through the Tee-Tree scrub, saplings and trees. Laughing and shaking, we gradually made our way up and, really, you could be excused if you thought this was just a crowd of idiots just making a lot of noise.

There was nothing to be seen in front of us except for the odd overexcited dog who was told to, "Get back here you crazy loon!", or similar good natured calls.

However, suddenly a rabbit popped up and could be seen scampering up the hill with its little white cottontail, bobbing up and over logs. Then there was another, and another! Until soon, we could see a great pack of rabbits scrambling to get away, but they were all heading into this corner. As each person followed up behind his or her now panicking rabbits, the netting was pulled over to close the gate. Then it was up to the brave people whose job it was to dispatch them.

I was sure I did not want to watch this mass slaughter, even though I had done my share of ending the lives of those little animals. As we headed back down the hill, the younger boys and most of the women and girls felt quite down.

Mum and I took great pleasure in a large clump of a flowering plant that grew there and nowhere else to our knowledge. A white flower looked very much like an Easter Daisy. We were sure that the Easter Daisy was not a native but it was a very strange place for such a plant to be growing. It was a fair way up a very steep hill and above where we found the pipe clay.

Perhaps there had been a cabin up there in the gold mining days and a garden planted there. It had done very well to survive for so long in those conditions. We picked great armfuls to take home to decorate the church. Mum would return often, when it was flowering, and take great bunches for fetes and church decorations. I wonder if it is still there.

The rush and excitement had gone on for several hours and when this was over we felt a bit of a let-down. All that remained for us all was to have a well-earned Billy tea and sandwiches. These were all prepared by the women and girls not able to take part in the drive.

I'm sure the men and other boys somehow washed their hands before tucking in. What happened to the rabbits? Well I did not really want to think about it. Of course, they were killed and were probably buried in a big hole somewhere. We all headed home for an early night. However, it had been fun. There is something positive about combining several people towards a common goal.

You could not imagine there would be any rabbits left, but it was not long before the next phase was begun.

The final and most successful program came next. It was the time for the Myxomatosis campaign. The farmer caught some live rabbits and took them to the Lands Department and the officer would inoculate the rabbits with the mix of virus.

The animals were then released into a heavily populated warren, and the virus was passed on to the others. It was a very virulent virus and it spread through the rabbit population in short order.

It was not long before the smell of dead rabbits was everywhere and rabbits blindly stumbling along were seen along the roads and paddocks. The virus fortunately, was not once passed on to other species. It certainly made a big hole in the rabbit population and rabbit meat is still eschewed by many because of it.

THE HARD-WORKING HORSE

Dad also used the horse for cutting hay by hitching the Lucerne cutter onto the back of the horse. Controlling the horse by reins, many hours were spent going back and forth and around the paddock until the Lucerne or grass was all cut.

This was a back-breaking job, as were many in those days, in comparison with today's methods. There may also have been a horse driven rake but I don't recall it. I do recall spending many hours raking the hay up unto rows and then building a stack with the pitchfork.

Another job for the horse, as Ken recalls, was to help in the building of a dam. Spring gully had a spring rising just half way up the gully. The spring water and rainwater would run down to the creek below. As there was little or no water in that paddock a dam would be an asset.

Hitching the big scoop onto the back of the horse, Dad was able to dig down, pressing the handles of the scoop and the horse pulling forward. When the top of the slowly rising wall was reached, Dad would tip the scoop up to empty it. Then back down and up to the top again, all the while guiding the horse with the reins and many verbal orders. "Gee up" and "Whoa" would of course be two used within the Australian wide vocabulary.

Once the dam was completed, a massive undertaking for both man and beast, it filled surprisingly fast. It was a great boon for the stock.

The horse was used then to plough a cleared paddock and then rake it so that a crop could be sown.

Whenever a heavy load was to be carried or lifted, the horse helped out. (Mum used to tell us how she rode around the hills on him.)

When wood cutting day came he would be a great help in snigging the logs down to the saw bench.

This same horse, after serving the family well for many years, became stuck with his back down in an old race, too narrow for him to turn over, and, unable to help himself, he was trapped there. After a few days of us all hunting for him, he was discovered in this position, but was unable to be helped up. Our faithful old friend lost his life there. On TV shows today, animals have been saved by having slings put under them and being lifted by a winch or crane. These, unfortunately, were not available in those times in our area.

DRESSMAKING

I made most of my own clothes, buying patterns and material on our trips to Bairnsdale. Having learnt the basics on an electric machine at school, I did all my sewing on an old treadle sewing machine at home. This machine was operated by treadling with the feet on the wide platform at the bottom.

The old treadle machine was gradually being phased out as women were able to buy the electric ones. The old Singer sewing machine was sought out for its design which was a very distinctive shape. As the years went by the bases became very popular as a table legs, often with glass on top.

In those days I was not too proud to wear homemade clothes, nor am I now. A few of the clothes I remember were a daring red poplin pinafore dress, with a very deep scoop front.

If I wore it with a shirt underneath, it was quite nice and respectable, and for the times I did not wear it over such things, I provided a dicky front. I sewed press studs around the front neckline and had various coloured pieces to attach to it to fill in across the front. I had a red one, a cream lace one and a black lace one. I made various coloured belts to match the fill-ins

I liked such outfits with different ways of changing the appearance and making it seem like a different outfit. I really enjoyed going through the pattern books and attempting something new. Most things worked out OK.

Many skirts in different styles and material were teamed with bought tops. I was never happy with sleeves in shirts and dresses, so I steered clear of those. Sleeveless frocks were OK.

There was another frock I made in a lemon fabric, much the same pattern but without the scoop neck and with un-pressed pleats in its skirt. I really fancied myself in this, especially if I had a tan to set it off. I liked being able re-use a pattern with slight changes and in a different colour. I made a plain mid-blue skirt, which I think now, as seen in a photo, was very long, but perhaps it was in fashion then?

This made the pennies go further.

For my engagement party I made a black and white hounds tooth check skirt with an inverted, mock pleat in front, into which I sewed black buttons. Putting in zips was a challenge, but was a lot easier than the alternatives. I added a mid-green twinset. This was ideal, as it proved to be perfect for the garden party evening.

When we were about thirteen or fourteen, some of my friends and I gathered at another friend's place to have a Sewing Bee. We all helped each other with any problems we might have. It was a nice after school and at weekends to get together and sew.

I also liked to embroider things like doilies and tablecloths and to add embroidery to an item of clothing. I made a lot of doilies and embroidered the flowers on them, then crocheted around the edges. Pillowslips were another thing I liked to embroider.

I enjoyed making trays with dead matches. They were all lined up neatly in any pattern on the board, a timber surround was added and finally a painting with lacquer.

CLEANING AND IRONING

At that time I was doing some cleaning and ironing at the boarding house, and a couple of other places.

I cleaned and ironed at this same friend's place the next day, and, on vacuuming the carpets, I found that the machine did not pick up the pins and I had to get down and try to pick them up from the shag carpet.

One day I asked if her mother was happy with my job and she said I was doing a good job but according to B, I did the ironing in a strange way. When I asked her in what way, she demonstrated and I thought that her method was strange. I guess it was the way your mother taught you.

My mother had finished school at an earlier age than I did to go full time as housekeeper at a wealthy person's house, and did domestic science at school before then. I would think that Mum would have been taught to iron correctly. I know that well into her eightieth year, she would even iron sheets and towels and underclothes. I always thought this was a waste of time. I had too many other more urgent chores than to do that.

The 'boarding house' I cleaned at was really just a dining room for the local saw miller's employees. The single millworkers would come in for a cooked meal each day.

This was cooked and served up by the lady of the house, who had a very large room at the back of her place. This was subsidised by the mill owner. It was my job to wash and polish this large room and the kitchen.

Another day I would clean at a farmer's house across the river. The lady was a full time nurse. These jobs at different times and days were very handy, as they brought in money to the household.

It also enabled me to buy materiel and patterns for dressmaking.

I would go straight to these jobs after school and Dad would collect me after his work. This also put a stop to other chores I normally did at home. Ken and Neil were now growing up enough to do some of them.

One thing I had to give up was my piano. I was learning to play and drew great pleasure from drawing out those beautiful notes. When I was starting to put the left hand in, along with the right hand notes, I really felt I was making some progress. When I could play some of the songs which I sang, I was ecstatic. I would sit at the piano, playing and singing to my heart's content. I'm not sure how the rest of the household took it, but I don't remember anyone telling me to stop.

However, with my cleaning jobs, home chores and homework, I was really finding it hard to fit everything in. I told Mum and my piano teacher that I could not continue, as my proficiency and intermediate exams were quite important and I needed to study for them. I was unable to give everything the best time needed.

Mum was upset as she really wanted me to continue to learn to play well, as she would have loved to have had that opportunity at that time in her life. She wanted me to go on. My piano teacher was disappointed for the obvious reasons. I think they were helping each other out as the money would have been needed in his large household, but he was able to teach me at a discounted rate.

This teacher and his family lived with us for quite some weeks when their house was burnt down. Their house had been up in the hills off Brookville Road behind Mr Simpkin's place where we had brought the sheep to be shorn.

At one time he had an old (converted army) tank with the top cut off and it was very strong.

It would push down a small tree and have good traction up and down the hills. I'm told my uncle, Mum's younger brother, even now recalls having fun on this vehicle during a holiday from Geelong, chasing around, and shooting rabbits from it.

After the fire, the family received a huge box of clothes from a charity organisation. We were able to let them have some of our outgrown clothes and in exchange, received some things from the box which did not fit any of them. I'm sure I have spoken of a pair of shoes I obtained from them at another time in this story.

I also believe I had a dark blue dress or coat, which fitted me. I was pleased to have any new (to me) garment as they would not very often appear.

Our friends did not build again on that windswept hill, but built a more appropriate home for the family size at the bottom of the hill, beside the road near Mr Simpkin's house. I remember being there when a team of volunteers were working on the house.

I was in charge of a child or two. I am not sure if it was my brother or one of the children in the new household.

At another time, we were not there on one weekend only. I recall digging and raking a very big garden bed. These people were keen gardeners as any friends of Mum's would be, and I believe a large number of dahlias were destined to go in there.

It is wonderful in a small country town how people will gather and help with building new homes, food, accommodation, clothes, and gardening and with anything else needed. When disaster strikes they are there.

I guess we all knew each other and had a good social rapport with the church and the regular social gatherings there and at the tennis club. We were all good friends.

Sheep Shearing

Another annual chore Ken remembers was to take the sheep around to a friends' place to be shorn. We had only a small flock of sheep and a family friend, Mr Simpkin, who owned a horse, came around to help round them up.

It was a large, steep and rocky paddock where the sheep lived. Having an experienced horseman was almost a necessity to round these animals up. The nearest shearing shed we could use was a long way away up on the Brookville road. Fortunately we were able to take a shortcut around the bottom of the hills. We all tagged along to 'help' but the most effective work was done by the dogs and the horseman.

After mustering more sheep from the cleared area, we would then go around the rockiest part and up to the top of the hill to round those little woollies up. Slowly we went, past Sang's Gully and Spring Gully, above the Lucerne paddock and past where we sawed the wood and into the next gully above Fraser's house. The hill where we had the rabbit drive yielded another four sheep and Mr Simpkin rode ahead to open the gate, with us trying to keep the sheep together.

"Look out Coral, there goes one!" As I dashed off to try and head off the one woolly, a few others decided to follow, as is the way of sheep everywhere.

"Get them Coral!" The boys yelled. However the sheep were too fast for me. Now we had two separate mobs going in opposite directions. The dogs yapped and nipped at their heels, but seemed to be doing the opposite to what they should.

The boys set off after one mob and I tried to round up the others. "Sit down you silly dogs!" We all yelled at once. Then "Go back! Go Back! Good dogs!"

The dogs suddenly seemed to have got the picture and the sheep were at last back under control. Except for one old ewe who had decided to put on her own lone rebellion. She turned around, chomping, teeth grinding and stared balefully down her nose at the dog on its belly trying to move her along. She chewed and stared some more then, with a stamp of her foot, she turned to follow the mob. Rebellion over.

"What kept you?" Mr Simpkin was sitting patiently on his horse, pretending not to have seen the shemozzle we'd just been through.

Through the gate, with the silly sheep jumping high over the imaginary something in the gateway, we moved along the rough road which had been scraped out for some unknown reason long ago.

Along the track we went and behind the houses on the Brookville Road, dogs barking, sheep bleating, people shouting and the horse putting in his own sound effects and the odd bird helping with the chorus. Up the hill, with more gates to open and close to the shearing shed. The sheep were herded into a pen where they would stay the night, and bliss! Mrs Simpkin came out to ask us in for a cuppa.

In we tramped with much discussion between the men about the state of the wool. The shearers were commenting on the lack of thistle in the wool, and forecasting a fair number of bales at the end of the day.

As the shearers were working on other farmers' sheep, we needed to keep out of the way, herding our sheep into allocated pens until it was their turn.

The table groaned with the usual country fare. The corned beef and tomato chutney, and egg and lettuce, along with the varied topped dry biscuits, were often passed up for the sweet cream puffs, scones with jam and cream, fruit cake and—*the piece de resistance*—a huge chocolate cake with whipped cream filling.

However, the hungry shearers, made a fair dent in the repast, along with several cups of tea. We prepared the sheep for the next day's shearing by sorting them into different pens. There was the usual chorus of dogs, sheep, whistled orders and yelling and dust flying, as always accompanied us in the shifting of sheep. We had heard the engine start and the buzz of the shears, but we didn't have to worry as they were not our sheep to be shorn today.

Usually the farmer who owned the sheep would help with the myriad of extra jobs other than the actual shearing. If a farmer was prosperous enough, he would employ shed hands and roustabouts along with the shearers. These farmers usually had their own shearing shed and would not have to drive them so far beforehand. Then again, some farms were so big that they would travel that distance and more to round up the sheep in their paddocks.

This was not usually the case in our area. Come to think of it, there were some large stations such as Bindi Station, 'Negoura' and some quite large farms in Cassilis fairly close to Swift's Creek. Ensay also boasted quite large stations, but not as large as the sheep stations in areas North West of us.

Having locked the sheep up for the night, we started the long trek home. Surprisingly it did not take as long as the trip out.

On arriving home our usual chores awaited us and we set to. Mum had a good meal for us and then we were off to the cot to get a good sleep before the early rise tomorrow.

Shearing day we rose bright and early, with the alarm not really needed as the excitement woke us and, outside, the rooster crowed and the birds set up the dawn chorus. After a quick but hearty breakfast, we got the essential jobs done, such as milking the cows.

As there was never a day that the cows did not need milking, that was our first job once the stove was lit. The kindling was piled on it to make sure it quickly reached the very high temperature required for the scones. Mum and I cut a mountain of sandwiches, baked the scones, and packed the dry biscuits and the different things with which they would be topped. The dry biscuits and scones would not be buttered and topped until needed as they would go soft.

All these were packed into tins and boxes, along with the cakes and sweet biscuits, all of which would of course be home made.

The makings for lunch, tea, milk and sugar were packed and the huge teapot was put in on top. Luckily Mrs Simpkin would have her fire going and a great hot water urn on top of it. We did not need to take some things as they would be provided.

As cars were going to carry the food and the younger children, we could get a ride in them this trip.

Arriving at the shearing shed, greeted by the always exuberant dogs, who, tails wagging, tongues out, were running around yapping and rounding us up as well as the sheep. We quickly penned the first of the flock inside the shed and made ready for the shearers.

Tar pots were lined up near the outside receiving pens, every scrap of the previous flock was quickly baled and the board swept clean. A slip was very easy on the lanolin polished smooth boards and the greasy wool.

The shearer strode into his pen and grabbed a sheep. Dragging it out, he had it sitting up on its tail like a good little sheep. Pulling the cord to set the shears in motion, the shearer bent to work. His hands glided gracefully through and the wool peeled back like a banana skin. There was no time to stand and stare as the belly wool was flipped out to be swept away by the roustabout with his broom.

Everyone had to be on their toes so as not to hold the shearer up. The belly wool off, the other shearer's wool was just fractionally behind. There was always competition in the shed between the shearers to see who would shore the most sheep in the day.

The shearer was paid by the number of sheep shorn per day so this also kept the speed up. Woe betides anyone who got in a shearer's way or held him up. It was his living so of course he took it very seriously. There may be a grunt between the two as they caught and dragged out another woolly.

Maybe the younger sprout would be sooling the older gun shearer on. He would maybe say that he'd beaten him that time but wait till a bit later in the day! Usually though they saved their breath for the very hard work.

The wool would fly as the men bent to their task, the sweat dripping off them and sometimes, reluctantly, they would need to stop to wipe the sweat from their eyes with the towel they always carried for this purpose.

Their backs would be bent in a painful looking stance and they kept control of the sheep with their knees and their other hand. The older smoker would have a ciggy stuck on his bottom lip and sucked it now and then. As each sheep was shorn it was let go into the pen in front and the shearer would swing around and head into the pens behind for his next woolly. In the time from when the shearer pulled his machine out of gear, and returned the two or three steps to his stand, the rouser had to pick the fleece and throw it precisely onto the table. If the rouser was lucky, there was someone else there with the broom so he did not have to run back immediately to sweep the floor of the remains of the wool.

If you were lucky, you could skirt a fleece and have it rolled and put into the wool bins before the next one came off the shears. In larger sheds there were enough people around to do each job without running or holding the gun up. The gun or gunner is the shearer who is very experienced and usually shears more sheep than anyone else in the day. All the shearers were treated as kings in the shed and plied with food all day and every day, at whatever shed they would shear in.

They would stroll in with not much to say and seem to stroll around, nonchalantly catching their sheep, shearing it, and working like clockwork all day to do their job. They were fed with sandwiches and scones and cake at every smoko. The meals that were put on at lunch time for them would amaze you.

I would wonder how they could bend over that huge meal and shear all afternoon and front up for more at arvo tea time. The woman of the house was responsible for the food and for having it ready on the dot.

The gear was shut off on the dot and started off on the dot. If the meals were not up to scratch, at any place the men would mumble laconically. "The meals weren't too crash hot at Old Billo's place last week." "Yeah," the other would reply.

That was probably all that was said but it soon got around and the women all pulled their socks up. I think it became a competition between them with the food. Maybe more was said in the pub at night. Most of the shearers were heavy drinkers and you would wonder how they could bend over all day with a headache.

I wasn't really caught up in all that. I would help out one day per year, when I was a teenager and sometimes helped with friends shearing.

CHICKENS

We always kept a good number of chickens. They were very good value as they could mainly be fed on table scraps and unwanted greens and weeds from the gardens.

They, in turn, provided us with very valuable manure for these same gardens. With the addition of a few layers of pellets and shell grit, we could reap a large number of eggs. These eggs would a very healthy addition to a meal and were a great help in all the baking which was done in the house. Sometimes if we had a few extra eggs, they could be sold to townsfolk. Chicken meat was a delicacy, eating it mainly on special days like Christmas.

Occasionally, if there were a large number of unlaying hens or too many roosters needed to be culled, we would use one for the plate.

Some would think that with a large number of hens around, we could have chicken meat often. This would not be good farming practice as it would be like eating all your sheep or cattle and have none to multiply and breed up. Something I am reluctant to relate, but was part of farming and something I still have a clear picture of is when the head of a chook was cut off, it would run around headless for quite some time. Thus the popular saying *"running around like a chook with its head chopped off!"*

It is one I use myself to this day and may be used by some with no knowledge of its origin. However the scene created a great laughing stock for the boys.

Plucking the feathers off was another task which we had to learn to master, or find it a very difficult job.

One must dunk the carcass into a drum of boiling water and wait for a short while, then pull out and pluck the feathers out. This was quite easily done if the correct temperature was used and it was dunked for the right amount of time.

Too long left in water too hot will result in cooking the skin which would then come away with the feathers.

Another sight of a fowl running about as though drunk now comes to mind. We had a few bantam chickens. Bantams were a smaller fowl, laying smaller eggs. They were quite a good prospect as they laid a comparatively larger number of eggs, though smaller, for the amount of food they ate.

Every so often we would have a broody or clucky hen. She would sit on a nest and would not get off without extreme persuasion by us. We would need to get the eggs out from under her as they were fresh and not suitable for hatching. She, being rather grumpy, would peck at us and even fly at us, trying to peck our faces. She wanted to sit on a clutch of eggs to hatch them out. In most cases the eggs would not be fertile or would be in danger of being inbred, so she would sit on them with no result. Usually we would exchange a dozen fertile eggs with other farmers. We would usually keep only one rooster. We didn't want inbreeding

Often a clucky hen was loaned to a neighbour. They may have fertile eggs, but no clucky hens. Unless the hen was clucky, she would not sit on the eggs long enough to hatch them out. The broody hen and her clutch of eggs would be kept away from the others so that she would not be disturbed.

Sometimes we wanted to have a whole new strain introduced to our flock. We would then purchase day—old chickens from a poultry farm. The fluffy, adorable little chicks, cheeping their little heads off, would arrive in a box on the bus which brought the mail and parcels.

Everyone wanted to see these little peepers, acting like clucky young women in the company of a little baby. Even though they could only be seen through a small piece of chicken wire at the top, there were cries of, "How sweet", "Aren't they gorgeous?" and "How soft and fluffy they look". However the box could not be opened until they were home unless we wanted to chase the fluffy yellow, black, black and white and brown cheeping babies in all directions.

It is amazing how quickly those tiny little feet could move. However once home they were released and out they would burst like bubbles out of a champagne bottle. They really were adorable, their fluffy little round bodies on the little stick legs and feet. They were put into a secure pen and given feed and water. It is amazing how they, only one day old, would peck at their special small ground wheat and drink from their water bowl.

Every now and then (I only recall seeing about three or four in my life), a bantam would take a fit and run around like it was drunk. It was usually a rooster and it was despatched as soon as it was noticed as it would have been unwise to breed from it or eat it or any of its progeny.

The eggs from our hens usually had a very rich, dark yolk as a result of them being fed plenty of greens. Because of the breed we favoured, we had a large number of brown-shelled eggs. These were thought to be much more beneficial to health.

This, I believe to be a fallacy these days.

Those rich dark yolks made for a rich yellow sponge, much prized by all.

DUCKS

However, a much better way to get beautiful high, dark yellow sponges was to use duck eggs. We kept a few ducks at times for this purpose, and others.

Ducks were said to be very helpful if let to run in the garden, as they ate the snails. Well, perhaps they did. However the good they did may not have outweighed the fact that they took very large bites out of lettuce leaves. They also made the paths treacherous with their droppings.

Ducks were usually allowed to breed naturally and hatch their eggs without being disturbed and when the mother brought them out for the first time they were a real hit. The fluffy yellow ducklings would follow obediently behind their mother flowing down and into the water like hot butter. Just like that often pictured scene that is used to depict ducklings. They were almost prettier than the more rounded little bodies of the chickens.

New Australians

One year there was quite an influx of new children at school.

Almost all of the men of the family began at Ezards Sawmills where my Dad worked at that time. It was a wonderful source of employment for many men in those days. It was the timber mill which made the town, providing work and building houses for many of its workers.

When the mill closed, many years later, Swift's Creek became almost a ghost town.

The Forestry Commission, with their many name changes and its amalgamation with the Department of Lands and Survey, provided employment for many and in the summer saw dozens more employed as fire fighters. There were still farmers and graziers, albeit living out of town.

Most of them lived in one-room huts up the gully behind the sawmill. There may have been two rooms in some huts, but little more.

The conditions under which they lived may have been quite basic but, I guess, a lot better than being in the war torn countries from which they came.

Their conditions were probably little better than my mother endured in those pioneer days. In spite of their primitive conditions, they were always very clean and neatly dressed.

Some of them came from the Balkans, and some from Holland. There were Greeks and Italians, and others from European countries. I believe that most of the Italians and some Dutch were sent to the Snowy Mountain scheme

Svetlana was a very lovely young girl as was her sister. With that distinctive beauty

I had not previously seen. Maria became one of my best friends and was part of the foursome who was always together at school.

Another Dutch girl, Betty, also became a good friend who lived closer to my home, where the Frasers used to live. We visited each other's homes and taught each other our language and other things that were unknown in our respective lives.

One very interesting thing to me was the way she used her needles to knit. The needles were a lot longer than ours and she would tuck them into her armpits and would knit away with great speed and correctness as she walked around. With my halting knitting being much slower and less correct, I greatly admired her skill. She also taught me some Dutch words, one or two of which I have retained.

Most of the young girls fascinated me in that they all wore earrings in their pierced ears. It looked very pretty and exotic on such a young girl. The new children fitted in seamlessly at school and learnt to speak English surprisingly quickly.

It was a real education for us country children, most of whom had never been out of the state. We really didn't hear much from them about their home country and the horrors and excruciating fear they had lived through.

One Dutch migrant family lived just across the creek along the track which we took as a short cut, when we could (creek allowing) to walk to church and school. The youngest son was about our age and joined in our escapades. He wore glasses and at school, some cruel children teased him and called him 'four eyes'.

We would be intrigued to see the women picking weeds and putting them in a basket. As we got to know them better and were able to understand each other, they said that we had wasted a very good food source over the years.

They would pick dock weed new leaves and cook them like spinach and thought them very tasty. They told us of other weeds we should have been using. I'm not sure if we ever did take them at their word and try their delicacy.

GEESE

Another bird in this category was the goose, which lived unpenned on the creek banks. I am at a loss to see what good they were.

I suppose they were good for keeping the grass down and, if you liked the meat, a substantial meal for the Christmas table.

Once again not a favourite with me and their angry hissing as they chased you was terrifying to me.

They were in fact short lived at our place as foxes could, and did, take a whole flock in one night.

TURKEYS

We also kept a few turkeys, huge birds, which took a lot to feed.

They were not a pretty bird in my opinion, with their wrinkly' turkey necks'. Their skinny red wattle which fell down over their eyes and their haughty faces didn't endear them to me.

Their feathers however, were very pretty with the black taking on a blue sheen.

Their 'gobble gobble gobble' could be deafening if a few of them got going after being startled, or maybe just because they could.

Maybe you can tell that once more they were not particularly loved by me.

SHIRE COUNCIL MEETING

One day our form was bussed to Omeo to the offices of the Shire Council to listen to a council meeting. All the councillors from each town came to attend.

We attended as part of our local government studies.

I don't think that any of us found it very interesting, except when a couple of councillors got into a heated exchange. I don't remember what about but it livened it up. Probably a clash between a councillor from below the gap who was opposed to one from above the gap.

Omeo was reached by climbing a very high hill. Some would call it a mountain. It was part of a range dividing the two towns. We had to climb via a very steep and winding road through a gap between to hills to get to Omeo. There was always great competition between the towns and people below the gap and those above the gap. Whether it was school sports, sporting teams, and schools, it made no difference.

It was thought by those below the gap that the base for the Shire Council should be in Swift's Creek and those above the gap thought it should be in Omeo. Fierce rivalry arose when players from below the gap player their counterparts from above,

In later years when a new Secondary School was to be built, both factions had implicit belief in their arguments. The Secondary school was finally built in Swift's Creek with students from above the gap needing to be bussed to Swift's Creek. This was much to the great disgust of the opposing faction.

However, back to the council meeting. The mayor, If my memory is correct, wore his robes of office with the councillors unadorned. After the furious debate there was not much council business that I can recall. There must have been a lot going on as we were all required to write an essay on our visit. I can't remember how many words were written but it must have been a few. When I won the competition, I received a very large attaché case with my initials in gold on it. It was a lovely dark blue and had

many compartments and closed with tabs and buckles at the front. It would easily fit foolscap size files in it. I also received a writing compendium, again with my initials in gold. It was a very neatly zipped folder which had writing paper and envelopes in it. I used both of them for many, many years and greatly appreciated such a lavish prize. My essay was printed in the local paper, so these many years later on I can truthfully say I am a published writer. I had forgotten that!

When I began writing again, poems, stories and this manuscript, I said to my daughter jokingly, "Who would think that I would become an author at my age?" She replied, "You need to be published to be called an author, so until then you are a writer!"

I was published years ago. **So there**!! I wish I had kept a copy for my scrap book.

School among the trees

In the front of the school were some very large elm trees. They had trunks at least two feet across. They had probably been there since the school had first been built in 1875. Around the base of the trunks were built circular seats. It was a lovely place to sit in the summer time.

Autumn brought the beautiful golden leaves giving the school ground a golden glow, and our feet swished delightfully as we walked through them. We all had the job of raking those golden nuggets into huge piles.

Some children took delight in burrowing into the piles, throwing them into the air and at each other. The leaves must have been carted away as I don't remember any fires being lit to burn them. In any case there was asphalt laid under the trees. They would not light a fire on that, would they?

As I have not returned to Swift's Creek for many years I don't know if those beautiful trees still stand, lending their shelter and shade to current children. I hope they do.

At the back of the school were two big peppercorn trees, something I don't remember seeing for a long time now. Beneath these trees, with their tiny red berries and their distinctive fragrance, were low stumps in the ground left from a previous building. They were just at the right height and size for our little rumps.

We sat there to eat our play lunch and our lunch, with every day Helen yelling "Dianne!" for her younger sister to come and get some of her lunch, which was always packed in Helen's larger lunch box.

We played this strange and gory game called 'Blackie'. I cannot find anyone who remembers how we played it, but it went something like this, "Blackie, Blackie, may I come in?" "Yes but take your boots off" Blackie would say, "But Blackie, Blackie my socks have holes in them" the other would reply. "Well take them off'" said Blackie. "But Blackie, Blackie, my feet are dirty". "Well chop them off!" came the answer, "But Blackie, Blackie, they will bleed all over your floor".

That's all I remember. How strange! We would, however, play that game for hours, every day, for ages.

Some children rode their horses to school. They were envied by many who asked for a ride. The horse owners were given strict instructions to not allow anyone to have a ride. The child would be almost certainly an inexperienced rider and may fall off and break a limb.

SCHOOL

Our school was very small, with two classrooms and a porch/cloak room.

Several grades were taught in the same room. It was a bit of a squash. When I first started school, we wrote on slates. I don't think anyone achieved a good writing style with those slate pencils.

One teacher brought us back to attention, if we strayed, not only with a ruler, but with it on its edge over our knuckles.

One chore which fell to me, by roster I think, was cleaning the inkwells. After we had progressed through the slate, the pencil and then the pen, we were excited to be allowed to use the pen. The inkwells were put into a small hole at each person's place in the desks. The first foray with the pens resulted in a lot of blots and blue fingers. An inkpot would probably be an antique these days.

The ink was mixed up in a big pot from powder with water added. The correct ratio was required or it would be too pale to see or too thick to run of the nib. The pens we used then were wooden with a nib on the end. The nibs needed to have the correct amount of ink loaded on them to do more than one word. And sometimes the nib, with a very tiny end, really was just one piece of metal with a slit at the end. These two end bits would become twisted and nothing could be done for them. They had to be thrown away. Blotting paper was needed to blot the word after writing it. The correct amount of ink was needed otherwise great blotches would appear on our books. Not popular with the teachers at all.

Another great lark for the boys was when they had a girl with long hair was sitting in front of them. They dipped the end of her pigtail in the ink!

Imagine the scream from the girl! The ink would most likely drip on the girl's dress too and would be a big job for Mum to clear up. The ink was not easy to get out of clothing. Depending on the age of the girl, a few girls had to do their own washing and ironing. Maybe the rest of the family's too.

We soon gained proficiency with the pen and mastered the swirling, flowing letters of the long hand writing. That script was very elaborate and when done properly, very decorative and neat. I still admire the old hand when I see it these days.

Unfortunately young children cannot today decipher anything written in 'running writing' as they call it.

The strap was also still used on the boys. Anyone misbehaving was sent to the head teacher, and, depending on his crime, was given the appropriate number of straps to his rear end.

A lesser punishment (perhaps) was the miscreant was given the strap on his hand in front of the whole class. I think the damage to his ego was maybe greater on these occasions

Milk supplied at the school was given to each child for a while but it was found that, having been delivered to the front gate, it would sit in the sun for some time. Of course there was then sour milk.

Another thing supplied to all pupils each Monday morning was a tiny iodine tablet as it had been discovered that that area was deficient in iodine and therefore the children would be too.

I never did hear of an underactive thyroid in that area, but I was much later diagnosed with an overactive thyroid gland.

First boyfriend

My first boyfriend at school was Peter. A very fun loving and cheeky fellow who was very attentive. We would sit together in the school bus with his arm around me. Looking back I find this very amusing given the later veto on going with boys. I guess we were too young for anyone to be worried.

We would meet again in the playground and make eyes at each other. What a happy and thrilling time, a girl's first love with such innocence.

VISIT OF THE QUEEN

There was great excitement throughout the school. The Queen, our Queen, Queen Elizabeth, was coming to Sale.

What fired us up more than ever was that we were going on the bus, then the train to see her. Wow! What a thrill. As the day came closer, the exhilaration level grew higher and higher.

The great day had arrived. We were so excited. The day had come at last. We all scrambled into the bus for the first leg of the journey. We got all the way to about Tambo Crossing when the excitement level was almost drowned by the boredom and some car sickness. Some children were sick, some getting sick and some about to be sick and most were getting naughty. The teachers had their hands full trying to keep the noise level to a dull roar.

We stopped and got out and stretched our legs and there was a long line to the toilets at the hotel.

The Tambo Crossing Hotel had been there since Cobb and Co days. A quick top-up for the bus and students and we were on our way. The worst of the bends were passed now and everyone was back to excitement and looking forward. As had been the case for the whole trip, the teacher kept up games of 'I Spy' and such to give us something else to think of.

Passing the 'Goat Farm' with no goats to be seen and on to the 'Red knob" where the banks on either side as we rounded the knob, were definitely red. A bit further now and up the last hill. Reaching the top of 'The Sand Hill' we could see off to the left a glimpse of the lakes. The church spire stood tall among the houses we could just see and the water tower was another tall landmark. Then, down the hill and we had reached Bairnsdale.

After another pit stop we all piled into the train, which had a long corridor on one side and compartments on the other with benches which would seat six to eight little bottoms. The trip to Sale was quite calm, as with eyes flashing everywhere, the students took in all the sights and sounds which was to most of them a new experience, as was travelling on a train.

At Sale we all piled out of the train and began running everywhere. We were free at last. After being cooped up in a bus and then a train it was wonderful to be outside. We ran, we laughed, we screamed, we jumped and danced.

We were then all rounded up by those clever and patient teachers and were marshalled to stand beside a road down which the Queen and Prince Philip was expected to travel. We were behind children who had preceded us, but waving our flags and jumping some may have caught a glimpse of the Queen's hat as she passed by.

It had been a very long trip to just catch a glimpse and the standing for quite some time had us all very sleepy on the trip back.

I don't remember anyone saying "What a letdown". I guess we were all too young.

AT THE HALL

As our school was getting too small for us, new classrooms were being built. Our grades, four, five and six attended our lessons at the supper room of the local Hall.

There seemed to be a less hurried pace to our days spent there. Maybe this was an illusion as we worked just as hard at our lessons.

There was a group of 'heaven' trees at the back of the hall and as they had a very distinctive, but not unpleasant smell, we liked to get among them. They had thin, long trunks and when stripped of the leaves made a very good pirates' sword.

Not only the boys got into this activity and I think there might have been a few minor injuries out of it. We chased each other around, having lots of sword fights, girls giggling and squealing, boys shouting and some rough language.

The injuries cannot have been too bad, because the teachers did not stop this exciting playacting.

It was at this time I was teased with the nick name "Captain Dimply Dimps".

One day I was crying (what a change) and the teacher asked why.

I told him they were teasing me with that nickname. He was probably trying not to crack a smile as he told me to be proud and relish that name. The 'Captain', was because I was school captain, and the other was because I had dimples in both cheeks.

The teasers were probably not meaning to be nasty, but I was, and am still very sensitive and took things to heart too easily.

Other nick names (one may be more distasteful) came into being when we learnt about the 'Coral Reef' as I was then 'polyps' for quite a while. Some, more to my taste were 'Coggles', 'Coralie' and' Empty Saddles', the last of which may need an explanation.

There was, at that time, a movie starring John Wayne, which we had probably seen at our weekly pictures. It was called 'Empty saddles in the old Corral'. Someone thought it was very clever to connect the nickname to the film.

We were all a bit sad to have to go back to our school again, although the thought of new classrooms excited us.

NEW CLASSROOMS

We had seen the new building take shape, with the posts in the ground and then the floor joists and bearers, walls rising and roofing going on.

One young fellow who was working on that job acquired the nickname 'Handle Bar Harry' as he had a magnificent moustache, curling up and out at each corner of his mouth, just like a handle bar. I was impressed to find that he was a cousin from Bruthen.

We were excited to return to the school with the new building finished with three new classrooms and two offices and a store room. Windows letting the sun and breeze in were all along the length of the building, with higher windows on the other side, in the wide, long corridor. There were hooks for bags and coats along the whole length with huge picture windows between the corridor and the classrooms.

Our peppercorn trees were gone as were our 'blackie' stumps. It seemed like we had all the room in the world.

These new classrooms were the newly titled secondary school holding all forms above grade six. Behind the lovely new classrooms, the area was terraced and planted and the old wooden facilities were gone. "What, no toilets?" you ask.

Of course our new cement block with three stalls for girls and the boys section at the other end, were built in the adjacent playground. Much to our delight they featured flushing toilets. What luxury!

The classrooms each had a wood burning heater which took the chill off. It was a very popular place during the winter. The boys were kept busy bringing wood in for each of them. The windows in the door of the heater were made of mica.

As it got older it began to flake and was of course not helped by little fingers pulling at it.

BROOKVILLE

We had a school trip to Brookville one year when there was snow on the ground.

Brookville was up in the mountains surrounding Swift's Creek. Log trucks were likely to appear around a corner, taking up more than their fair share of the road. These logs were taken to the Swift's Creek sawmill. The road was very steep, winding and narrow.

There were many tracks cut through the bush to allow the log trucks to get into where the trees were cut down. Another very important reason for these tracks was to allow access through the almost impenetrable bush in case of fire.

Very few people lived on that mountain but it could not even be called a ghost town as there was no town. There had been a saw mill there but it was now closed.

The bush always fascinated me but the tree ferns in the moist gullies were extra special. Their beautiful arching six foot or more fronds wept down to the trickling stream and the many glorious species of ground ferns. Some were dainty, tiny fronds, and others were strong and tough looking. They all defied their look of fragility as, when the snow lay some feet above them, they survived to burst forth once the snow was gone.

The ground was carpeted in soft, delicate mosses. One would be excused for thinking that a tiny fairy might suddenly appear in this veritable fairyland.

The melodic trickling of the stream down over the moist mossy rocks, the tinkling sound of bell birds, the imitating call of the lyre birds and the cheeky cheep of the smaller birds, all portrayed the bushland scene.

Nature unsurpassed.

ALONE IN THE BUSH

Lucy Strobridge had turned her back on society, living in a hut with a dirt floor. She scared people away by slamming an axe into trees and making eerie noises.

All this was effective as 'Mad Lucy' had everyone too frightened to approach her. Many were curious to see her, but her antics kept them all away.

She had turned her back on society many years ago. A documentary film had been made some years ago, but I don't believe the reason for her life as a hermit ever became known.

She was rarely seen, but sometimes she was sighted flitting from one tree to another, keeping watch on any one who ventured near her chosen patch. One person she trusted was a log truck driver, who would pick up her box with her order for groceries. The order was packed at the store and the same man left the box in the same place for her. Her writing was quite neat and legible. One could almost forecast her order. It would be almost the same each week. As I handled that order many times during my stint at the store, I could, even now, remember what she would order and how many. Even now, as she has passed on (as I learnt by my research into that area) it would be inappropriate to disclose these personal facts. Occasionally Lucy would ask, in her order, for a dress.

We, at the shop, knew what size she wore and would obtain a cheap cotton dress from Bairnsdale. It appeared to be all she wore all year around. The winters would be a challenge for her as snow often lay thickly on that mountain. I hope she had a huge fireplace in her hut which could accommodate huge stumps.

The 'Brookie' Falls

On another trip to Brookville that we made we had a Sunday school picnic. It was summer and up in the mountains it was much cooler. Every year we had a Sunday School picnic, trying to find a different venue each year. We usually had running races for both children and adults. It was usually beside a stream so that we could go swimming.

This year it was at the Brookville Falls. Several cars drove up to Brookville and across the paddocks as far as we could go, then trekked in to the 'Brookie' falls. The falls fell twenty feet or so into a large pool at the bottom. We picnicked beside the stream at the top of the falls. The only thing I really recall was Bev saving Ken from going over the falls.

Ken was playing in the water between the rocks. Suddenly he was being swept towards the drop. The current was much stronger than expected and he wasn't strong enough to pull out of it. Everyone started yelling and running around in a panic. Mum was yelling "Someone get him!" There were people running in all directions, along the bank, in the water and over the rocks.

As Ken was gradually picking up speed towards the edge, he realized his danger and started yelling, "Please! Help me! Help!" Bev raced along the bank and jumped onto a large rock quite near the edge of the falls and as Ken was being swept past she made a grab for him, and missed.

Everyone gasped. Mum just stood white faced watching her son being swept toward the falls and almost certain death. Bev jumped to the next rock and reached out and, "She's got him!" came the cry from a dozen throats. Mum burst into tears of relief. "Oh Bev" she said, "You have saved him. Oh thank you, thank you". As Bev half carried the terrified boy to his Mother, he started to cry and shake. "Wrap him up. He's in shock" said Auntie Con.

We all stool motionless, unable to believe that a boy had just nearly died, for that drop would have killed him, even if he had not landed on the rocks surrounding the pool below.

No-one felt like eating, or playing. All in shock and feeling quite ill, we packed up the picnic, piling everything willy-nilly into packs and bags. We all then headed back to the cars and home, still not really believing what had just happened.

Not a pleasant ending to that year's picnic

NUNNIONG

Another trip into the mountains was up to the top and high plains of Nunniong. We set out quite early to climb, albeit by vehicle, the mountain from which the Tambo River had its source

The bush was close to the narrow road all the way up to the top. The trees were mainly eucalypts and many of them were huge and the log trucks, which could appear at any time from around the very tight corners, would be loaded to the hilt with similar sized logs. As they required the whole road to negotiate those tight corners, it was nerve-wracking thinking that they could be over us with no warning.

I have always loved the bush and each individual tree had a shape and form all of their own. I feasted my eyes on all this green beauty, but it was not entirely enough to make me forget those very steep drops at the side and the imminence of a log truck full of huge logs suddenly upon us.

The little fern filled gullies were a verdant delight. The tall weeping tree ferns gracefully and exquisitely dripping down to trickling water. The tiny dainty ferns gave a beautiful, lacy edge to the tinkling stream.

The road wound around the side of the mountain, sometimes on the sunny side and then on the shady side. Almost to the peak was a large bunker set into the ground in case of a bush fire and tracks leading off to still another logging site. We needed to walk the last steep track to the apex. At the peak was a fire tower, which was manned twenty four hours a day in the summer fire season. A narrow very steep ladder led to the building on top of the tower.

I, along with some others, was very nervous climbing so high above the ground, albeit slowly. We pulled ourselves up, step by step until, on reaching the top, we stepped through a hole in the floor of the hut on a stick. All around were large windows, looking out over endless hills with nature's patchwork of green.

A spark from a lightning strike, its tell-tale smoke just a thin thread at first, could be spotted from the tower, giving timely warning via radio to the control room in Swift's Creek.

I could not imagine how anyone could sit up here in this eyrie alone for twenty four hours of the day. Of course there would be a roster to keep it manned. It was almost worse making our way down that ladder and I for one was very glad to feel solid ground beneath my feet.

We all trudged back down to the vehicles and set off on another track which finally fetched us up onto the Nunniong High Plains. We were amazed at this large stretch of plains so high on top of a mountain, with mountain grasses which would be covered by snow during the winter, not growing very high. Perhaps they had been eaten back by the large mob of brumbies which lived up there.

These magnificent bush horses were rounded up by some men who caught them and tamed them, broke then in and sold them for a profit. It was quite a rough way to earn a living, but those horsemen were tough.

We roamed over part of the plain and came to the narrow, slow flowing stream, meandering its way snake-like across the plain. It was the source of the Tambo River. It was difficult to imagine this stream which was only two to three feet wide so that we could step over, was the wide faster flowing stream and sometimes huge and violent river which made its way past Swift's Creek.

Having eaten our packed lunch and ran around and stretched our legs, jumping back and forth over the stream, we piled into the vehicles and set off.

Reaching the track which led to the lookout, we took another, beside which was a log hut. This was the famous Moscow Villa Hut which was a popular place to camp. Being made of logs, it was just a fairly large room with I think, some log benches and a really large open fireplace, big enough to roast an ox.

There was a narrow walking track beside a stream and, a huge surprise to me, a big area of sphagnum moss. I used sphagnum moss in my potting mix and for the bonsai trees I grew. It amazed me to see it there in its natural habitat. Something I had never thought to find.

Once more into the vehicles and now we were heading down the mountain. It was a very steep and narrow track with corrugations which nearly shook us off the road. Coming out above Ensay, we passed the Ensay sawmill and Ensay Hotel.

After a pit stop at the Ensay Hotel we re-joined the Omeo Highway now known as the Alpine Road.

With us all feeling weary by now, the final few miles to home were spent maybe snoozing or in a blur, with not even the often praised view from the top of Connors Hill being enough to excite our senses.

Mount Flagstaff

A lower mountain of those surrounding Swift's Creek was Mt Flagstaff or 'Flaggy' as it was popularly known. Flaggy was just behind the school and was a fairly popular hill to climb. There were numerous lower hills as this was close to the Great Dividing Range. Although it was reasonably easy to climb, the last few feet were a challenge. Those last few feet were very steep and quite difficult to climb. The route we would take started from behind the school and virtually straight up with no variations. We would, for some reason, climb down, a different route, coming down at the Football ground.

Later it became much easier to climb 'Flaggie' because a track was made up the side, starting up just past the mill. The track was not built to make our climbs much easier. In fact I am not sure if I ever did climb it again after the track was built.

'FLAGGIE' AND OUR TV

The reason for the track was due to television. With a tall tower for the antenna, a generator, and a bank of batteries, the advent of these objects enabled us to view television, albeit black and white and 32 volt.

One needed to have a 32 volt television set and a generator and batteries similar to the ones we had not long installed at our place. The town was able to have electricity long before we had that modernity, because the power was generated via the mill which needed power to run it. It had sufficient energy to enable the entire town to have electricity.

As we lived approximately three miles away from the town, we were quite a bit behind times. Because we were not a rich family, we all needed to save for a while to afford that square-eyed box. When we were able to afford a set, there was great excitement in our household. Although we were only able to get one channel for many years, we were soon hooked on our favourite shows.

However, we still had our TV free days or nights. Usually Saturday nights were game nights. On these nights we had a family night and the TV was not switched on at all, irrespective of anyone's favourite shows. Even Dad's news was not viewed that night.

RADIO

Before the advent of TV, we all enjoyed our favourite programs on the radio (or the wireless as we called it). Even after TV tried to rule our lives, we still tuned into our most loved programs. We had a battery operated model for many years with a big square nine-volt battery. I believe some are still around for those outback places that remain without power. This type of battery still powers some big torches.

'Blue Hills' was a very popular program, not least in our household. Even though we had very few idle moments, we would find some task with which we could occupy ourselves whilst our ears were busy.

Ironing was a fairly quiet job with which we could stay relatively close to the radio. Darning, an ever present task which we could take on without guilt, was usually carried out at night whilst hearing the children's' times tables or spellings.

Another very popular program was 'Pick-a-Box' with Bob Dyer.

Songs and singing

Music was something we really appreciated on the wireless, as that was often the only way we could hear it, except for hymns at church and our own voices.

There were a few player pianos around and whenever we were able to visit a home which had such an instrument, we would all delight in a sing-a-long. Everyone would join in and sing out loud unmindful of who might be listening. Sing-a-longs to the radio took place more often, as that machine was more prevalent then. Some people had the gramophone along with the Bakelite record seventy-eights which were played on them.

The gramophones were all wound up with a handle plugged into the side with which the instrument (or machine) could be wound. Music was very important to us as a family and we would all take delight in most genres.

As time went by, we were able to have a piano. Mum was able to play enough to pick out a tune. In spite of stopping my lessons, I was able to do the same. When we had someone visiting who could play, we always prevailed upon them to play. This would invariably become a singsong.

One year there was an amateur-hour night at the hall.

Most of my family took part in this and enjoyed it. Mum, Dad and an uncle took part in a skit. 'There's a hole in the bucket dear Liza'. It was very popular and scored highly. I had been practicing with a guide leader some of the songs which we performed. Her voice was contralto and mine soprano and we sang duets in harmony.

'Whispering Hope' was one which I really loved singing with her. I am not sure what the other was. I also sang two solos of which 'I'll walk with God' was one, I think. However, much to my delight, I won and was told my voice was suited to the microphone and I should look to singing in clubs and such places. As there were no such places in our area, I took on board the compliment, but disregarded the rest. Night clubs? In Swift's Creek!

MOUNT BURT

The lowest mountain amongst those which surrounded Swift's Creek was Mount Burt.

Lower than 'Flaggie', Mt Burt was not so hard to climb. It was on the opposite side of the valley to the other we had climbed on the first page of this story. The hills down which the fire was trickling were on your left, looking from the road to 'Emoh Rou.

These we climbed fairly often, but Mt Burt to their right, was, for some reason, a larger challenge. What the end of this climb almost always resulted in was joining the Omeo Highway at Taylor's straight. We would have arranged for someone to pick us up there as we really didn't want to walk into town all sweaty and windblown and red-faced. A beautiful cold drink would go down well though.

The difference between hills and mountains is a rather grey area here, maybe It depends on where you live, or were brought up. The other side of Mount Burt gradually morphed into farming land and a good fox whistling area.

Hotham is an excellent skiing area. It was reached by going up the through the gap from Swift's Creek via a steep winding road towards Omeo, through the township of Omeo with its long steep street. The Hospital is perched high on the hill past the historic building of the Omeo post office in the centre of town and out along a very corrugated gravel road over a small but swiftly flowing stream then out past Cobungra Station. Continuing along to our right were the mono colour buildings of Dinner Plains, not then but now in later years.

Mount Hotham is the highest mountain in our area, part of the great dividing range.

As we got further up the mountain, the snow got deeper. We had, as was recommended before starting out over Hotham, checked with the weather report and if we needed to carry chains. They had said that they didn't think we would need chains today. We were going over to Ken and Julie's wedding which was Easter time and usually there would not be too much snow on the road that early in the season. We were slipping around a bit and I was getting a bit concerned. This had been my first trip over Hotham and, with the fog which had gradually got thicker and thicker, it was very eerie.

THE SNOW GUMS

So out along the bush track grow
Its ill shaped branches, in the snow
from howling gale would bend and forever be misshapen
to hide in ghostly hue so as not now to be axed and taken
to make some shelter for those who go
and trek through those mountains high, we know
not when, we know not when they might be taken
whose shelter from the ice and snow
had thought not now of how in mountains there
the diminished stand of wondrous ghostly snow gums
axed are now, even now, to boil the pot
with those ghostly gums gone now forever
axed till all the trunks whose beauty bare
were lost to future loving eyes, like mine, but never,
never even now in retrospect but at least by me forgotten not
the wondrous sight, the beauty of, the camouflaged, but not
completely hidden
were there for me to see, the snow gums vain attempt to hide
assuming now
The white snow's hue and did survive for many countless years
for my loving eye to see as though bidden
through my greatest fears to see
the beauty of the snow gum tree. *Coral Boucher*

The higher we climbed, the snow came down more thickly. The markers which told the depth of the snow, were becoming harder to see. There was a very steep drop on one side of the road, and the other was a high bank. Needless to say we stuck as close to the side where the hill sloped up higher than us, as the fog. snow and slippery road made us very nervous. Dad was a very competent driver and we had all faith in him. As we climbed higher, we would have had a wonderful view as we came to several lookouts if it had not been for the fog. We neared the peak and looking ahead we could see our route. We had no alternative but to travel a very narrow road which dipped down very steeply for a short way. This might be OK on a clear, dry day, but unfortunately the fog had cleared just enough to allow us to see the horror before us.

The road looked barely wide enough for us to drive on. To make things worse it looked like a knife edge with a very, very steep and *lo-o-n-g* drop on each side of the road. I just wanted to get out and walk.!! But, because of the snow, I would probably have slipped off the edge. Slowly, slowly we inched down the road, the car whining in high gear. Dad must have been as afraid as we were. He did not show it, except for his fingers. They were gripping the wheel tightly and were WHITE!

We all gave a huge sigh as we got past the dangerous part. All of us wanted a pit stop at this stage and to have a hot drink and to be able to stretch our legs. But these were not available to us at this stage. The rest of the mountain was kinder to us. Still travelling slowly, we negotiated the winding, steep road and survived. We stopped at a small clearing at the foot of the mountain. Warming up with a cup of tea from our thermos flask, we all breathed a sigh of relief.

What an invention. We all praised Dad for his wonderful driving and for bringing us down that mountain safely. Had we known how bad it would be, we could have taken an alternative route. We did take the lower road on our journey home. One good thing about that horrendous trip was that we had no cars coming down as we were going up and vice versa.

A wonderful time spent with Ken and Julie, and their friends and relatives. Julie put on a wonderful meal. One of her recipes which I filched that day is still a favourite with my family even now. It is so easy to make and so tasty.

Needless to say we returned via the lower route as the snow was still on duty at Hotham. It just goes to show how fickle the weather is up in those mountains.

BUCHAN CAVES

Another less challenging trip was to Buchan to see the well know limestone caves there. The caves were well worth looking at and still are today.

The time we went, the two smaller ones were closed. However we excitedly made our way up the gully to the larger one. As we entered I felt a slight shiver, a bit afraid of the unknown and also of going underground. The stroll through was fascinating, providing you are not claustrophobic. The stalagmites and stalactites were beautiful, dripping the water which over the many, many years had shaped them.' They were like ice carvings, crystalline and iridescent and almost translucent. As we walked between large pieces jutting out and up to a narrow opening, I was becoming a little worried, but, moving along through that narrow gap, the colours of the outcrops changed and some were almost wavelike. The underground adventure was well worth it, going deeper and deeper with the colours and shapes changing all the time. It was hard to believe it was real. After having a picnic lunch under the trees we made that long trip home.

A Happy Interlude

One time I remember with joy, which sounds strange, because I had my tonsils out and spent some time in hospital. I was approximately eight years old. For the first few days I had a very sore throat but remember mainly the ice cream and jelly I ate for most meals. It was a great treat for me then as we had very little of these at home. The main reason for my good time was the hospital secretary, a Mrs Cracker I think, who allowed me to play in her office. There was a huge cupboard with toys for children so it was like several Christmases had come at once. I was the only child in hospital at first and few other patients. I virtually roamed the hospital at will and was the darling of old ladies and staff alike. I would often sit in a comfy chair in her office and write and draw. Towards the end of my stay a boy named Bruce came into hospital. He was very ill, having had a mastoid (behind the ear?) operation.

I found out later that she was actually a cousin by marriage.

SWEET LARCENY

Dad and my uncle used to collect honey from wild bee hives in hollow trees. Dad and Uncle Clarrie armed themselves with all the necessary equipment before they set out. Like all good robberies, the hive was usually sussed out before-hand to make sure it was worth robbing and what tools were needed for the job.

Good sharp axes were a must. I can imagine the men gnawing slowly, taking some time to get to the softer half—rotted wood towards the centre of the trunk. Sometimes a whole section of tree was taken home. Not a good thought there as the sleeping occupants would come along too and, waking from their nap, would be off with an angry roar, aiming for the most vulnerable places on those noisy robbers. The job needed to be done rapidly. The next essential was the smoke can and several sugar bags with some sort of scoop to scrape the comb out. Nets were needed to go over the robbers' heads plus long sleeved cotton shirts, tough trouser fabric and gloves. Wool was known to be a bad choice for gloves and jumpers. The bees seemed to be on the attack with that fabric. Maybe with a looser knit, it was easier to stab their deadly stingers in.

Now, having trekked in through the bush and found their quarry, they set to with the jam tins full of green leaves and a small amount of dry material. The dry material was set alight and once the fire had caught on the green leaves, the latter emitted great clouds of sweet eucalyptus-smelling smoke.

The smoke tins were waved around the whole area, hoping to get every one of those hardworking insects off for their nap. You will have gathered that the smoke would make the bees sleepy so that they would not attack the robbers. Great lumps of honeycomb were put into the ever handy sugar bags after brushing the sleeping bees off. Sugar bags were filled with that delectable treat. After trekking back through the bush they would load all the gear and their spoils into a vehicle. Home would come the hunters.

One day, when a fair hunk of log was brought home, bedlam broke out. "Oww Mum something bit me!" shouted Neil, "And me!" Came a chorus of exclamations. "Look out Clarrie there's one on the edge of your net!" The cat, with an agonized *Yoo-wl* dove for cover under a shrub and the dogs woofed and yelped and danced around not knowing which came next, the woof or the yelp. Every one ran in all directions. "Hey Mum, one's got under my shirt! Oww!" "Look out George there's one crawling near your ear!" With the sailor s' hornpipe and Irish dancing all rolled into one, the tune was more like banshee's wailing than Danny Boy. The sleepy bees were waking and wildly stinging every one in site. The robbers themselves, still having half of their protective gear on, were far from safe with the bees coming out of their sleep. No-one was safe. The screams would slowly die away, with the odd louder one again, so we ran for the blue bag. The blue bag described earlier was a good antidote for insect stings. The thing with bees was you needed to get the stinger out, which the bees had kindly left with you. If that was not taken out, the swelling, pain and itch was much worse. The thing was—I don't know if anyone told the bees that they died once they had lost their sting. They may not have been as keen to bite then. After all having had a piece of comb and honey, minus bees, and a few more coatings of bluebag, the sugar bags were hung from a hook on a veranda or tree. Beneath the bags were half kilo drums to catch the honey.

The comb with a little honey in it, freshly reaped from the bush, was food of the Gods. The bags of comb would be hung there for at least a week. The honey would flow out and leave the comb to be gradually eaten as a sweet treat. The honey was put into glass jars for later use. There were always a few jars of our precious condiment for fetes or street stalls.

LARYNGITIS

One time when I was in senior school I had a bad bout of Laryngitis. I was unable to get further than a whistle. It was very difficult when a teacher asked a question of me, I could only whisper.

I got out of a few chores then, but my voice came back after two or three days.

NOT AN ANGEL

One day I blotted my copy book (not literally) at school. A boy was giving me some cheek, during lunchtime. It must have been cold because we were inside. This boy was a relation by marriage to me and was always giving us cheek. I was chasing him around the desks when a school teacher walked in.

He said "Any resemblance between you and an angel is purely accidental".

He then gave a wry grin and walked out again. It's strange that I still remember this.

DEBUTANT BALL

When someone put on a Debutant Ball, I was not sure if I would be able to make my debut. It had always been said that I was not allowed to go to dances or anywhere with boys and not allowed high heels or makeup. I was not even allowed to sit with a boy at the pictures, until I was sixteen. We young ones would all sit at the back and some boy/girl friends would cuddle up. One boy tried to work it so he sat with me. I was too afraid of what my Mum would say. I said "My mum would kill me". Who knows, a different decision and my life might have changed then.

The deb ball changed all that. Maybe Mum thought that I might not have another chance to make my debut. Nevertheless things changed. I could go to practice nights for the debut. I think we had chaperones there.

I was to have a lovely white frock, made by a friend of my mothers who was a wonderful seamstress. The frock was long and had a very full skirt, held out by hoop petticoats and many starched net ones. It was a flocked net and was sparkly. My partner was to be a young man who had lived across the creek, but now lived just out of town on the Omeo Highway. My parents and I discussed it and it was decided to ask him. He was a good clean living young man who drove a ute with two large milk vats in the back.

The vats had taps and it was easy to fill the diverse receptacles the housewives brought out to get their milk. He was a very good footballer and had got best in the league, best in team and had a lot of trophies. We practiced our dance and other dances for the night.

Once the debut was over I was allowed to go out, with him and we became very good friends. I would meet him at lunch time from school, which was conveniently timed for his milk run to finish then. We would sit in his car in the middle of town, in front of the shops and chatted each day. We went to the pictures on Tuesday night and went to Youth Club Dance on every other Saturday night.

He was very polite and good natured and did not drink or smoke at that time. He had a meal with us one night each week and stayed for supper. It was the thing in those days and I had usually baked lamingtons, Ginger Fluff, chocolate slice and scones. After supper when Mum and Dad had gone to their room, we sat and chatted for a while.

For some reason, I would be very sleepy and often dozed off. This happened quite often and Mum often remarked about me coming home from work and drooping around 'like a dying duck'. It may have been early stages of my present condition.

It must have been very trying for J.

One night, after being out at a dance, we had spent a short time cuddling in his car. I did not stay out for long, as I was very tired and it was cold.

After I had been in my bed for a while and almost asleep, there was a knock on the door. I got up, put on my dressing gown and went to the door, hoping to keep Dad from being woken. It was my uncle. I was surprised at him calling so late at night. He asked if Dad was there and I said he was asleep. I can't remember if he insisted on seeing Dad, or if he had gone away. It was very strange.

I asked J if he had still been sitting out in his car when Uncle had come. He said he had still been there. When asked if Uncle had seen him in the car, J said he didn't think so. I realised how bad it must have looked. Maybe Uncle had thought that J was in the house with me, with me obviously having been in bed. I was worried at what this would do to my reputation.

There was nothing more said about it, except for my aunt saying one day "We know what goes on behind closed doors". I was worried for quite a while and asked J not to sit in the car for so long after I had gone in.

I may have been very tired but I was always busy, either in the garden, or in the house.

I remember being down in the paddock near the creek mowing away with the lawn mower. I used the scythe to cut down the bracken fern. I scythed it so far then used the mower, tipping it up and gradually letting it down to cut it from high till low. I believed that with less bracken fern, there would be more grass for the cows.

Anyway, we made our debut and had a fantastic night. He and I continued going out to the pictures and dances. Every year there was a Footballers Ball. We and all our friends usually went and J almost always got another trophy. He was very popular with every one. He was like an Idol figure to the younger boys. He was a star footballer. He was in the scouts and became a leader. He didn't drink but somewhere along the line he took up smoking. We were boyfriend and girlfriend then and would go for a drive on Sundays.

SWEET SIXTEEN

At last! I was sixteen. This was a very exciting birthday for me as it was ruled that until this age, I was not allowed to wear high heels or makeup of any sort, even though my friends were wearing both before now, and I was older. I was not allowed to date or go anywhere with boys.

I had started work at the bank when I was fifteen and I was beginning to know my way around the duties there.

There was a youth group which had a dance every week and I was at last able to go to that.

To add to this excitement was the deb ball. I had been allowed to go to strictly chaperoned practices for the debut, but until now I was still made to stick to the rules.

It was only a few days after my sixteenth birthday that a teller at the bank suggested I should go into the Miss Australia competition. I laughed at him and said "What, here in Swift's Creek? Not me. Anyway what about Rene?" who was my best friend and his girlfriend. He just laughed and said I looked very like Tania Verstac who was a 'Miss Australia' around then.

Whilst I had laughed at the suggestion, I was secretly pleased and flattered. It had given me quite a boost. No one else had ever complimented me on my looks by then. I was a very shy person, who made her own clothes, so I was very busy. I was still ironing and cleaning at three different places after work.

I played basketball (netball now) on Saturdays and was a defender, because of my height. I would love to have played centre or attack but the girls who played there were much faster than I.

I later played goalie because there was no one else. I was not very good there, but the team needed another goalie. I threw the ball off to the other goalie whenever I could.

We played in Ensay, Omeo and Benambra. It was not much fun playing in Benambra when snow lay on the ground. The footballers revelled in it and as it was still snowing, played in deeper snow.

They thought it was great fun.

Sports and Social nights

We all kept fit as a family by partaking of many different sports.

We played quoits which is now a popular game on shipboard cruises.

Another game played with quoits was deck tennis where we threw the rope quoit over the net. I cannot remember any rules now but remember having sore fingers as my nails were too long and the quoit would often catch my nail and bend it back. I don't know if I learned my lesson and had my nails shorter for the games after that.

We all enjoyed these games played in the masonic hall.

We also played volley ball at school but it was introduced towards the end of my school life. I recall that I really enjoyed it but did not play very much.

As a family we often played cards with friends on a Friday night. Some nights they would come to ours and others we would go to theirs.

Mrs S. did not play 500 card games, but she always enjoyed teaching my youngest brother to play cribbage. I made a cribbage board with drills to do the holes and stained it with green walnut juice.

We played with this at home for many years.

I always remember the very tasty supper she provided. I eventually went out to help her and sometimes did it all myself. It was very simple, just chutney and chopped bacon and cheese on fingers of bread. These we put into the oven for a while for the cheese to brown. They were very tasty.

LEARNING TO DRIVE

Learning to drive on those winding, narrow often steep roads should have made me a good driver. The roads were often gravel and often had rock falls.

One time, as I was just learning, I was concentrating on changing the gear, but J said "Good, but what about that wattle tree in front there?" I slammed on the brake and said I was sorry and that it was hard to do two things at once. Little did I know. It was only a baby wattle tree too.

We continued with the lessons week after week when I was the right age to get my licence. I don't think we had learners then.

He took me for my test. The policeman would have seen me driving for quite a while with J and asked me a couple of questions, took me out to the car and we drove up to rubbish tip hill for a handbrake start. Everyone went there for that test so we had practiced it very often. Then back to the station and he asked me to look at some signs across the road and said, "That's it, only thing is you must have your eye glasses on when you drive".

I was astounded.

No three point turn or real road rules questions. It was amazing.

It was only because he had seen me wearing my glasses at the bank that he made that restriction.

It was many years later, and the only time I wore my glasses was to drive. Sometimes it would be quite a hunt to find them.

My husband at the time happened to mention the fact of having to wear glasses to drive with no proper eye test to the local policeman. He said, "Send her along to see me". I went and with only a short eye test, I was able to drive without them.

LEAVING SCHOOL

When I was fifteen, the headmaster went to my parents and said, **"This child** needs to go further in education", and that I was intelligent enough to go to University and that it would be a shame not to allow me to do so. Dad said that, "No daughter of mine will ever be a nurse" probably because of the sights and sounds nurses were subjected to during the war.

Dad said that in any case, he had two boys to educate, and you didn't educate girls as they just go off and get married. He said I was required to get a job and contribute to the family expenses. I did get a job and I did contribute to the families' expenses and yes I did get married quite young. So he was right in one respect. Because in those days you did not go to work once you had a family to raise.

Banking

The bank manager came to the school at the end of my Intermediate year and chose me to fill the staff vacancy they would soon have on the marriage of the girl I was to replace.

Coral's First Day at the Bank

Beverley was a wonderful inspiration and taught me all she was able in the short time until she left. We sat up on high stools at a big desk secreted behind a huge partition which kept us hidden from the customers. This building was perhaps one hundred years old so complied with those customs.

We needed to mentally add the columns in the huge ledgers. Not one erasure was allowed in the ledgers so a lot of care needed to be taken. We were required to very neatly put a line through the error so that the figures underneath were to be clearly seen. Any error at all was frowned on so extra pressure was put on us try harder. We also sorted and carefully checked all the cheques.

These had to be carefully compared with the signatures we had on record and check to if enough funds were in the account. If not, we would dishonour them i.e. they were sent back with a note on the back that read 'Present Again' if there were not enough funds to cover the amount of the cheque. We then sent them to all the banks from which they came.

Before I left this job we did progress to an adding machine to add the cheque totals and the account balances.

One bank manager was nicknamed 'Flat to the Boards' as every time a customer asked how he was he would reply with this comment. He was a very fussy man and was always scuttling around the office and needed to greet all the rich and powerful men of the town and kowtow to them.

When the bank was being rebuilt, the old one had been there for many, many years, we operated from the empty shop across the road.

The tellers would perform their duties further up the very long counter, towards the door, with huge safes and filing safes separating the managers' office and our work area from the public. This shop had been a grocery store, hence the very long counters.

One day one of the tellers, having had a prior late night, was not feeling too well. All of a sudden, there was a huge and sickening thud. It sent shivers up my spine.

I had never heard such a sound before. Whipping around and feeling sick to my stomach, I saw this teller on the floor. He was flat on his back, not moving. I just stared at him. I was in shock. I'd never seen or heard a man hit a wooden floor like that. Just in a dead faint, with nothing to break his fall.

The manager yelled at me (I'm sure he had to yell to break me out of the shock) "Coral get a glass of water!"

As I ran off to oblige, after him repeating himself again, I needed a glass of water myself. My heart was racing and my hands were shaking. When I returned with the water, the teller had regained consciousness and slowly stood up. He looked very pale and looked as if he could easily faint again. I sank into a chair and should have been treated for shock myself.

He was sent home to sleep it off. I was not present when surely he was reprimanded very severely. After all, bankers had a position to protect and were required to be circumspect and set a good example.

Another time I had sprained my ankle playing basketball, as it was then called, and having limped to work, I was installed in the makeshift manager's office for that day and several days afterwards. Seated with my foot up, it was really a treat as we normally had to stand all day to perform our duties.

We moved back into our newly renovated bank with a modern staff room and we didn't hide from the public at desks any longer.

I was permitted to help customers then if the tellers were too busy.

We could stand at the counter with glass topped openings for this purpose. In those days women were never promoted to teller.

COURTING

When I worked at the bank, my friendship with J continued, with me meeting him, as before, almost outside the butcher shop. I'm sure in retrospect, there would be a book being kept. Will he kiss her? Will they cuddle? We did progress to a quick cuddle and a quick peck on the cheek as we parted. We were now acknowledged as boyfriend and girlfriend and as things warmed between us, our Sunday drives were taken away from prying eyes. I would, during the footy season, have tea at his mother's table after the football and my netball. He would then take me home afterwards.

He would eat at our place one night a week.

Engagement

When we became engaged it was after all the correct protocol of J asking Dad if he may court me. Mum and Dad agreed to our engagement, providing we waited at least twelve months before getting married as I was only nineteen at the time.

The engagement was announced, with a big party in our back yard. We had a very good turn up with a lot of my aunts, uncles and cousins coming to share our happiness. There were also many of my school friends, J's friends, Mum and Dad's friends, neighbours and church people. I made myself a black and white hound's tooth skirt with which I wore a bottle to emerald green colour twinset. I can't remember what the evening consisted of, but I think there was a bit of trying to dance on the close clipped lawn. There was, of course, a groaning table of many different types of savouries, slices and several sponge cakes and a pavlova. Mum and I were kept busy for days and even weeks in advance if a product would keep that long.

There was no alcohol, as we were a wowser family. Dad may have had a beer on a hot day after working hard, or a little social drink. At least there were no thick heads to my knowledge the next morning.

WEDDING DRESS

We went to Melbourne to buy my wedding dress, which in itself was a cause of great excitement. I had rarely, if ever gone to Melbourne before. We visited several bridal gown shops and I tried on so many dresses, it was beginning to be a bit tiring. Then we found it.

This frock was my dream gown. It had a long, very full skirt which was held out with stiffened net and a hoop petticoat. The bodice was tight fitting and the waist dropped to a 'V' in front. It was a beautiful white lace and the long lace sleeves just made it right. It had a pretty neck line. Then I tried on the veil with it. I felt like a princess and Mum's eyes were filled with tears. Fortunately I was able to afford that one so we went home happy.

WEDDING DAY

The big day had come! It was the 13th of April 1963. We were to be married in the Methodist church in Swift's Creek. It was the church in which we had worshipped all our lives at 'The Walnuts' but it had been moved into town.

I had had my hair permed a week before the wedding, thinking it would be settled down in time. Big mistake! HUGE! It was just a frizz as all my perms were then. I had always had trouble keeping my hair tidy and looking nice. So thinking it would be less trouble on the day and on our honeymoon I had opted for the dreaded perm. Perms have always been a disaster for me but I go back again after a time, thinking things would have improved. Other girls had soft wavy perms and they looked lovely. Why not me? Yuck! It was a disaster and the look of the dark haired princess I had glimpsed in Melbourne was gone. Stolen by my yucky hair! It was even lighter. I was not to show every one that princess on that day.

However, let me continue. Relatives came from Geelong and Melbourne and there were a lot of people there. The bridesmaid's dresses were beautiful. They had lovely full skirts, sweetheart necklines and the colours were pink, lemon and mauve. The girls, my best friend, my cousin/sister June and J's sister all looked lovely. The service was beautiful and I was so happy that I think I was in a daze and cannot remember much of it. I had married the man I loved dearly.

We went back home to change and there was confetti everywhere. They even found some in the outside toilet. I regret that I had taken such a long time to change and collect my bags.

My uncle and his wife had to bring their twins home as they badly needed a sleep. I'm blessed if I know why it took so long, but it did.

When we returned to the reception in the hall, the food was all ready. Catered by one of the clubs to which mum attended, it was a feast.

However the excitement did not allow me to eat and then we were off. Off to Adelaide, my first time out of the state. We stayed in a room in Glenelg, just on the beach. Not very good beach weather in April, but we took long strolls, picking up lovely shells along the way.

We drove into the Adelaide hills one day and they were a great delight. The problem was the unbelievable traffic. We did not realize that we were virtually passing the Oakbank race course there on a major race day.

Another day we travelled to Elizabeth and passed Kangaroo Island. We opted not to go over there for some reason. All too soon we needed to head home, travelling along the lower coast road. It was a wonderful journey.

Coral's Wedding with Dad

RENOVATING

Once the hoo-hah of the party was over, Dad and J's Dad set to with a will to make the very old house on the dairy farm habitable. The house had very high ceilings and, probably for costs sake, they were reduced to a more modern height. Just as well because it was a very frosty area just there on the river. It would have been so much harder to keep it warm. The kitchen with its slow combustion stove and later the lounge with its slow combustion heater, were the only warm rooms in the place.

The windows were all cut down to suite the now lower ceilings.

J's Mum saved all her egg money for a long time and with it she was able to buy the bath and hand basin and maybe the shower base. We were so grateful to her for doing this as there wasn't a lot of money around.

Mum and Dad bought the lounge suite and the kitchen table and chairs. This was a wonderful effort by them as they paid for the wedding and both families were contributing towards the material needed to renovate the house.

The old house had hessian dividing the rooms. This was replaced with Burnie board.

Being so old, maybe at least one hundred years, the boards on the outside had huge knot holes in them. When I painted it, many years later, I had to use a fence paint which would soak into the timber and not show the puttied up knot holes.

As the house had been many months without a roof, the rain on the old flooring boards had buckled them and when it came for floor coverings, there was a lot of sanding going on.

There were many weekends spent at our future home with Mum and Dad, J's Dad, maybe J's brother, J & I and a family friend who was very proficient with the building of the cupboards in the kitchen and bathroom. We all helped as much as we could and J's Mother's contribution was her afternoon tea and often dinner for us all. J's mother was a very good cook, having worked as a housekeeper to one of the local families. The house had only the lounge, our bedroom, the bathroom and kitchen lined. I believe I bought the stove as my contribution from my low wages. I saved very well, as did we all in those days.

Some rooms were still not painted when my daughter was christened. The one bedroom when the first born needed to have another room to make way for the new baby in the cot, was only lined then. Not painted.

There was no money and very little time to be concerned with a minor thing as house paint. Finally, quite a while after the third child came, I was able to paint all the walls inside the house.

When I had started work, I can't recall whether I paid a nominal board or none at home. Mum had said to me that she would only take a small bit (or none) providing I put that extra amount into a savings account for the future.

We had a smaller wood heater in the lounge room at first, but later, when I was able to work between children, I bought the big slow combustion heater from my wages. At first, we had a kerosene fridge but I am not sure where that came from. Likewise the bed, although I have a faint inkling that it might have been in the package of kitchen, lounge and bedroom furniture.

We were very lucky having had so much given to us. I had a low wage and worked extra hours after school and work. J did not earn very much then so I don't think we would have managed nearly so well without help from our families

How hard working and frugal they were. On looking back, it must have been a battle for them.

'Willow View'

I fell in love with the willow trees along the river at the back of the house,

In midsummer, they wept to the ground, providing shade for us, for cows, for geese and for dogs, but I will admit that I never did encounter a cat there under the willow trees. The beautiful trees even provided food for the poor starving cattle when there was no other food for them. As everyone knows, dairy cows need a lot of green feed for the production of milk. During the drought, the willow trees were one of the very few green growths around. The chain saws lopped off some of the branches. I watched with trepidation thinking that my beloved trees would be ruined. However everyone needed to give something up to keep the stock alive. Come spring though the delicate green, tiny shoots would be weeping to the ground like green lace. No not ruined, definitely not ruined. A little different, but the same weeping shape as always. They played their part well.

The willows, I heard to my dismay, were being taken from the river and stream banks. They were apparently blocking the streams and causing havoc during the floods. Surely this was not a case that warranted the death penalty?

Another use I found for the willow, was to cut its very long, thin twigs and whilst they were green, we could weave baskets out of them. All sorts of baskets, big or small. They were so very handy.

With me being a tree lover from way back, I must grin and bear the times when their beauty was repaid with such cruelty. I am a tree lover but not a tree hugger and always see both sides of the story.

MY HOME

Willow View became my home and I enjoyed setting it up to the best of my ability. Some of the rooms were lined with Burnie board but some still had the hessian hanging between the rooms. The kitchen and our bedroom were painted, but everything else had to wait.

When it was time for our firstborn to move out of our room to make way for her brother, we managed to get the one bedroom lined. We had a slow combustion stove in the kitchen through which water was piped to be heated for baths and cleaning. We had no electricity. We had a battery run radio in the kitchen and every day at lunch time, everything stopped for us to listen to Blue Hills. Even the men folk enjoyed that story. Probably the reason for the success of that program was that it portrayed everyday life in Australia. We really missed that program when it came to an end.

We had a wind-up gramophone on which we played our records, singing along and dancing to the tunes.

I enjoyed baking still and enjoyed trying out new recipes for meals as well as cakes and biscuits. I continued all the things like jam making, butter making, bottling fruit, making sauces, tomato and plum and bread making. All the things my mum had taught me and on which I had worked at home with her.

I darned socks but, regrettably, not very well and my husband used to say they were too uncomfortable. I think it was the thicker wool I used which made the darns bulky. Using the mushroom, which was what we called the device we put into the sock under the darn so we would not stitch the two sides of the sock together. It also held the darn up nicely for you to work on. Working diligently, I wove the wool across one way then wove the other way over and under the other wool. Never mind, I did try and some passed muster. It was a lot cheaper than buying new socks when they developed a 'spud' on a toe.

At Christmas we kept with tradition and decorated the house, almost always substituting something else for the traditional holly and pine tree. We would hunt along the river until we found a suitably sized and shaped tree. Sometime it may be a branch or a small wattle or kangaroo apple or whatever we could find. We always had plenty of mistletoe from our favourite big tree at Boucher town.

My mother-in-aw taught me her method of baking scones using sour cream. As we always had an abundance of cream, even if it was not sour, I would put a spoonful with vinegar or lemon juice mixed into it. These scones were very popular and if bread was short, I quickly knocked up a scone loaf to cut sandwiches from.

When the stove was very hot, if noticed by my husband, the cry would go up "The oven's hot how about a batch of scones?"

I was looking after my sister-in-law's children after school whilst she worked. I remember baking fifteen dozen biscuits per week. I admit I made the biscuits small so that they did not have as much. But I think this backlashed as they would take more. With my three children and their three I had six hungry children to feed after school.

I did the same with fruit. I would buy small apples, bananas and oranges so I got more per kilo. It was a real blessing when there was fruit on the trees. It's a shame we could not save the fruit in fit condition to eat raw so we had to make do with our preserving and freezing.

SUCH PROGRESS

Eventually we had 32 volt electricity installed in the two houses on the farm, with banks of batteries to provide light, but the engine needed to be started if we needed to wash, with our new 32 volt washing machine or iron with our 32 volt iron. This sounds as if we dashed and bought all the new machines at once but in fact we had to gradually replace our out-dated appliances with 32 volt electricity ones.

We still had no television, but eventually we had a 32 volt fridge to replace the smelly old kerosene one. One of the most horrible things I was glad to replace, was the kerosene heater. Always smelly, even reeking, it was almost better to be cold than light it. Really though, the extreme cold on frosty mornings was too much.

So, over the years we replaced our old appliances and added new ones. I even had a 32 volt Mixmaster.

Then at last we had television. What a marvel. In black and white and only one channel, we needed an inverter to pick up the signal from flaggy. It was a snowy and unreliable picture, but it was a great novelty for us. A group of local men had set up a receiving station on top of flaggy with banks of batteries. Unfortunately the batteries would go flat and the whole thing required a great deal of maintenance by those dedicated men and one in particular I believe.

MAH-JONG

On one trip to Geelong to see our relatives there, we called in to see my uncle Neil in Sunshine. We played Mah-jong then with them. They had recently had a trip to china or someplace where they played that game, and learned it there. We really enjoyed it but had been unable to find a set anywhere so that we could play it. I have completely forgotten anything about it now.

We stayed overnight and went to Uncle Neil's work with him in the city. We could not believe the trek he had to make each day. We would get onto a bus near his place and travelled a short way, then caught a tram to another stop. We dashed to the next tram going our way and then literally ran from that tram, down the street to catch the train which took him into the city. Another tram trip ensued, then, at last he was at his work. I really was amazed at the literal dashes people made each morning to get to work.

WEEKEND OFF

One weekend we decided to take a trip to Sorrento to see J's very good friend. 'Pommy' had a fairly new wife and we loved her. We thought how well she suited 'pommy' and how devoted they were. We went to the movies and saw 'The Big Fisherman' and thought it a wonderful show, far ahead of the ones shown in Swift's Creek in those days. We then had a wonderful ice-cream called 'blue heaven' one of approximately thirteen special flavours they carried. All made on the premises I believe.

Another day, J and I took the ferry across to Queenscliff. The water was rather choppy and I did not enjoy our short voyage that day and after a stroll along the beach, found ourselves running late for the ferry. Quite a dash it was to the finish but we made it by the skin of our teeth. Our hearts pumping and breaths heaving we sprawled onto the ferry seats. We'd made it! Phew!

One of those days on our stroll along the beach, on climbing the sand dunes, there before us was, oh goodness!! What a shock! There were men in army uniform everywhere. The army barracks! We had walked into the back of the army barracks

We took off and scrambled back down the dunes as fast as we could, fearing we would hear a "Hoy! What do you think you're doing there?" We thought we would be in very great trouble, maybe even locked up, to be in such an area. With hearts pumping we made our way back in much more haste than our leisurely stroll out.

THE FARM

Things were getting worse on the farm with year after year of drought. The men worked even harder on the farm, trying to keep things going. They contracted to cart hay and sometimes to bale it.

The irrigation sprays were going almost 24 hours a day, with the spray lines needing to be moved often.

The motor over the river ran the pump for the sprays and needed to be fuelled up often.

One bonus was, if you were interested, the annual horse races were held just back across the river from where we would be working and we were able to hear the loud speaker with the race calling very clearly.

We didn't need to go to the races. The children, in later years used to walk up along the river the next door neighbour's place to see the horses run.

THE DAIRY

We all put time in up at the dairy each day with very little return. It was backbreaking work in that we needed to lift ten litre buckets full of water to wash down the cowshed floor. The most unpleasant time was when the cows had been eating fresh green grass. You would be crouched down putting the teat cups on, then SPLOSH! A green laden tail whipped across the face. You can imagine how we felt let alone how we looked.

Some of the bales had a hook to which we could attach the long tail. Others didn't. Some of the tails had been cut off for this reason. A practice I deplored even if it prevented a green face pack. Anyway it was probably good for the skin!

During the summer the flies were bad, bothering the cows and us. The manure on our faces would attract them too. The heat was very bad in the tin shed in the afternoon. It was harder still when the children would be down in the river having a swim. One good thing about the very early rises in the morning was that it was nice and cool compared with late afternoon.

I may have upset people sometimes when I said "Farming's a mug's game".

If I was talking unknowingly to a farmer they may have though that I was inferring that they were mugs. I was however, referring to the fact that we were at the mercy of the weather. If it was a good year, the cattle were fat and plentiful and you couldn't sell them. Or if it was a bad year, you didn't have stock to sell.

In the bad years, you would get rid of extra beasts so that you would not have to feed them with the very scarce food available, or they would die of hunger.

Some farmers would shoot their stock rather than see them starve to death. When food was very scarce, great loads of hay would be trucked in from more fortunate areas.

I would concentrate more on the vegetable garden then as it provided the food for our table. I also trapped rabbits for us to eat and to sell. I made bread and butter, sometimes being up until midnight, pulling the last of eight or nine loaves out of the oven that I baked per week for the cut-lunches the children took to school.

Any extra fruit, tomatoes and some other vegetables were bottled and later, when we had a big freezer, I would freeze what I could to keep us going when those products were not able to be grown.

J continued to play football and was a real star. He was named best and fairest and best in the league, year after year. It was a delight to see him play. There would be a scrimmage of players with the ball somewhere in there, then, suddenly, out of the pack ran J, football under his arm. A rover, he was a bit shorter than others but he was almost the fastest in the league. J often had bad football injuries.

One year he had cracked ribs, another a smashed up face. I am a bit reluctant to say, but it was often a case the opposition trying to slow the best down.

J became a trainer or 'medic' if you like when he was unable to play himself and was also coach to the junior team. I also continued to play netball and later coached the junior team. As you can guess, football and netball ruled our lives in the winter and J was a very good cricketer in the summer. I used to be scorer for those matches.

J was also in scouts and then became a leader. He was idolized by the younger boys.

MY GARDEN

My garden, as opposed to Mum's garden, was always a joy to me. It was a very much needed stress relief. A huge area was taken by me as I branched out with vegetables, whatever the season. Always a gardener, as taught by my garden-loving Mother, I planted shrubs. I planted bushes. I planted bulbs. I planted trees for fruit trees for shade and trees just for their beauty.

I tried to keep vegetables for each season to keep us as self-sufficient as there were the most terrible frosts in that area. We were very close to the river and my friend, just around the great sweeping corner, was also a great gardener and just as close to the river but did not get the same degree of frost than we did.

When I was not busy with my many chores, I could spend all day in the garden.

I did it all including digging holes for twin pools at the front of the house. The small pools were surrounded by rockeries, using the soil I had removed for the pool. I planted rockery plants and herbs on the small terraces topped with twin weeping cherries (well not quite twin as one was pink and one white). I added fish to the pools to keep the mosquitoes down. This was one project I really enjoyed and was pleased with it when it grew and did what I wanted it to do.

I had a large fernery at the side of the house with the beautiful ferns being another of my favourites. The slats at the top kept the sun off delicate plants and keeping to a lesser degree the frost from the frost tender plants. These slats also were a frame for grapevines to flourish on.

There was a beautiful old tamarisk tree at the front of the house. It was such a wondrous site when in flower with its pink lacy fronds weeping to the ground. In spring it was almost aping the willows with its delicate green lacy branches, a truly beautiful tree.

CUTTINGS AND PROPAGATION

I always had habitually broken a piece off a plant and put it into soil to grow a new plant. Now I did it with a purpose. I would take maybe ten cuttings from a plant, put them in the ground, then the same with many other varieties. They would nearly all grow. How easy.

I was given a book by Jack Plumridge called 'How to propagate plants'. I treasured that book and consulted it very often. I built up a large collection of potted young plants.

I even obtained a business name, 'Tambo Valley Plants'.

I began selling from my fernery. I would have dearly loved to set up a nursery, growing seedlings and young plants. I had a great number of perennials which were so easy to break up and make more plants from.

Sadly, I did not have the courage to give up my work and put the time in to make it a true nursery. The money I earned then was badly needed in our household. I made my own potting mix from well-rotted compost, sand and water granules. For my orchids and ferns I needed Oak leaf mulch. There was an abundance of this just over at J's parents place. I always used to take a shortcut and hop over the fence and climb down a slope to get it.

The old plough bit back

However, this day, the old rusty plough on which I had stood myriads of times, decided to go on strike and bit back at me. Down I went and the plough blade cut. I felt the place and there was a great hole under my slacks in behind my knee. It didn't really hurt at first but it was a great shock to feel that great hole. I tried to walk but couldn't. I yelled for help and luckily J's father heard me. He was starting to panic.

They laid me on the couch and when the bush nurse came, she found that the stocking I was wearing under my slacks had got pushed into the wound. There was little blood although it was very deep because there was a lot of fatty tissue there. They said if I had been really skinny it would have been much worse. The fat had provided a layer to keep the plough blade from going into the bone. They took me to hospital lying in the back of the station wagon. By that time the pain was getting bad.

Arriving at the hospital, they took me straight into theatre. The doctor took hours to stitch the wound from the lowest level to the top, probably a good two and a half inches in. As he finally stitched the last layer he said how lucky I had been to have some fatty tissue there. He said he didn't think I'd be wearing any bikini after that. I was in the hospital for quite a while because the plough had years of rust on it and I developed an infection.

Then another infection set in and they needed permission from Canberra to use a special drug to treat it. I had to lay with my leg uncovered with the sun coming through the window onto the wound. When my leg was uncovered, no-one was allowed in the room except one special nurse. All this hoo-hah was because of the infection.

When I finally got home I could not wear slacks, and, it being so cold I wore long skirts. Luckily I had two I had made to go to balls. They were made out of very narrow corduroy. I wore these for quite a while even when I went back to work. When I came to wash the stockings (or pantyhose) I had worn on the day of the accident, there were no holes or runs in them. Only (how gross) big lumps of fat. I still have a very horrible scar but it is high enough up on my thigh at the back not to show.

TREES

The poem I wrote, 'First Love' was a slight hint to the reader of my greatest love at that time, which was trees of all shapes and sizes. I loved trying to grow mock bonsai out of seedling Japanese Maple, potting them carefully, regularly trimming their roots and wiring and training the branches.

I loved this tree in all its seasons. So graceful, and so colourful with its autumn foliage and the dainty, delicate spring foliage and its red stems. Always so beautiful

I was not the only one to love the Japanese Maple as a family of goldfinches used to nest there and on another branch. The firetails would also nest and return each year, whether the same hen and husband or maybe a new wife. Who knows or cares? I'm happy to have shared my tree with those lovely creatures.

I found myself looking with new eyes at each tree with the differing, shapes and colours and for certain trees with certain attributes.

I even loved the eucalypts with their different coloured tips. We would take in the myriad coloured tips when flowers were a bit scarce and with a flower or two, make a wonderful display. I tried with little success to draw the differing trees. It certainly wasn't for the want of trying.

FIRST LOVE

When I was just a girl I fell
Totally, irrevocably, and forever I fell
In love with trees
Trees in all seasons
Trees for all reasons
Strong, majestic and tall
Even when they are just small
I fall, in love with trees
With beautiful blossom or autumnal hues
I fall in love—in love with trees
In all their glory I choose
Their pale coloured trunks of red or brown
Their branches spreading out or down
I fall—in love with trees
Poets adore them, singers sing of them
And I? I love them
In forests among their peers
Or alone standing tall
I love them
Trees bringing joy, trees bringing tears
I love them all above the rest
Gently cradling the smallest of nests
Home for many a creature small
There is nothing so good at hiding them all
So, love them I will
The trees and I, are at rest *by Coral Boucher*

HOT HOUSE

When I had more money, I purchased a hot house. I used this to put all my frost tender plants into during the winter.

The frost would even get the orchid leaves and often kill them. Winter was a heart breaking time when beloved plants would be knocked and die. One should have been used to coming out one morning to the death of tomato plants, zucchini plants, squash and capsicum. The flower garden was always a trial and error as most people did not have frost as severe as we did there on the bank of the river. We were just before a big bend and my friends around the bend would not have any as bad as we did. One soon began to be sure of the hardiness of different plants in our particular patch.

The hot house was not enough to protect some things so I ran a fan in there to try and keep the frost off. On very frosty nights I put two kerosene lanterns in there, and, with the help of the fan, a lot of plants were saved.

GOOD NEWS

Some months after our wedding we were thrilled to tell our families the news. We were expecting! We had jumped around in excitement ourselves and found it hard to keep it a secret for a while in order to wait and be sure.

We had decided that we would have our children whilst we were young so that we would not be too old as they grew up. We planned to have three and decided they should be two years apart. Nature does not always fall in with our wishes, but we were lucky. Our second child was born two years after our first but that's where mother-nature needed to show us who was boss. Our third child waited until our second was four years old. We were and are delighted with them all.

We had a wonderful time, going to dances and balls and playing cards with friends. The balls were the real thing with the girls all wearing ball gowns and long gloves and the men suited up looking very suave if uncomfortable. With some of us the gowns were homemade, often a long skirt with a sleeveless top. There were three or four couples who we played cards with, taking turns to have the sessions at each other's place.

We were very happy then as I had been all my life. I was a very avid reader. I read only at night unless I was ill or it was raining and I had decided to give myself a few minutes break from my many duties. I would read at night no matter how late we had been out. I always read even if only a page or two. I believe it stopped me worrying about anything which had happened during the day. It was a great stress buster and it relaxed me.

I have always believed that children should be encouraged to read. I feel it increases their word power, their spelling and grammar and shows them another part of the world rather than the one they are in.

The book mobile came each week or two and it was a great boon for us readers. It was a free service and the big bus was filled with books. Literally a mobile library, I used to exchange books for my father-in-law at one stage.

My husband did not read at all except for the papers. My eldest son does not read now. My daughter does when she can find time (very rarely) and my youngest son will read occasionally.

As always, I find that I am never bored as I am happy to read now I'm retired.

WEEKEND OFF

A few weeks later, football and netball over, we decided to drive to Paynesville to watch the speedboat racing.

After a good day watching and exclaiming over the races, we headed home to milk the cows.

However, we were not to milk the cows that night because our world came apart.

We were driving slowly along, discussing the boat races, when we saw a car dash across the road out of a dirt road from behind long grass. Almost stopping, we exclaimed at the stupidity and then I saw another car close to our bonnet. I screamed and J tried to stop. There was a terrible crash and there were things flying at me including glass.

When I came to I was on the floor of the car. I looked across at J and screamed his name. I thought he was dead. Then he moved slightly, which put my mind at rest.

Seat belts were not required in those days, so we had both been thrown forward.

I could hear voices outside the car now saying something about losing too much blood and not waiting for an ambulance. I was carefully lifted into the back of a car and someone was asked to "Keep an eye on her' and J was put in beside me. I was aware that I had lost control of my bladder, but that was the least of my worries now. The next thing I remember was being on a bed or stretcher in hospital with someone stitching my face.

The worst things were the needles as the anaesthetic was injected. I had eighty five stitches in my face that day. I was very lucky as one cut went right across my eye, from my cheek over my eyelid, through my brow and into my hairline. I had another across my forehead which had a flap hanging by a small piece of skin. It was hoped that this would heal properly and not need a skin graft. There were other cuts across my cheek.

J was kept in overnight for observation. He only had a small cut across the bridge of his nose.

The worst part of my few days in hospital was the vomiting as morning sickness had kicked in. I would need to sit up with my head bent over a bowl. The pressure on my cuts was very painful.

The first thing I asked about was the baby alright as I was two months pregnant with my daughter. They said we needed to wait for a few days to see if I would lose the baby. It was a terrible wait until they said it looked like I was lucky to be so early along. Then it was a very long wait until the baby was born and hoped she had not been harmed.

Police came to ask questions. I said that we were only going slowly but the car had appeared from nowhere without stopping or even looking, just intent on racing behind the car in front. We just could not stop in time. However, they were going very fast. I heard someone had broken his ankle and another had a broken finger. However the policeman's son who was driving was not injured.

The boy with the broken leg came to see me in hospital and cried and said he was very sorry and that it had not been our fault. I now have scars on my face, which are gradually fading as the years go by. My children have never seen me without scars.

When I needed to be taken home by car, I was a nervous wreck. If there was a car anywhere in sight, I would stare at it, my whole body tensed up, until it was gone, then burst into tears. It was worse if a car was coming onto the road from a side road. I just cried. The same thing occurred even if a car was miles away.

I gradually got better and I was able to drive and be driven. Strangely enough I was much less tense if J was driving the car as opposed to anyone else. I guess it showed how I knew that he was not at fault and I trusted him completely. That doesn't mean I wasn't very tense, but not as much as when driven by someone else.

Life went on with morning sickness everyday.

One of the things which plagued me most was the scar which had run into my hair. I was told that the nerves were knitting together, but it drove me mad. It was like beetles crawling in my hair. One night when we had friends over playing cards, my scar started itching. It was hot in the room and it itched so much. I just burst into tears and ran outside, scratching and crying. My husband followed me out and I said

"I don't know what to do! I just can't stand it".

At that he lit a cigarette and gave it to me, saying it could help. I took the cigarette and puffed at it. It was my first ever puff at a cigarette. How foul! It almost made me sick.

It was a toss-up as to which was worse.

I persevered with the cigarettes and they seemed to help. The itching became almost bearable. I was two months along with my daughter then and knew nothing about not smoking when carrying a child.

That began twenty years of this addiction and I dread to think of the harm we did to our darling children in those time. I was at last able to give it up with the help of the patches. It still required great determination and willpower. I wish we had known the effect on the unborn in those days, and the effect of smoking in the car with children. It was never given a thought, but I am so very sorry now.

The scars on my face healed some and I was sent to Melbourne to a plastic surgeon that realigned the scars and reduced the keloid scarring. I was one of the unlucky ones who healed with lumpy, bumpy skin called keloid scarring.

Many people said I should have gone back as they could do much more with scars now. I said I had got used to them and couldn't afford it.

There are many things I experience now which are resulting from that accident, some of which have been passed on to my daughter. People say I should claim for them, but the case is closed and could not be reopened.

The insurance company had held the case open until our daughter was born and it was ascertained that she had not been affected by the car crash.

All my medical expenses were paid and the car replaced and I was given one thousand pounds for pain and suffering. They said if I had not been married, I would have got a lot more, but I had 'caught my man'(their words) and I was OK.

Birth of first child

At last the day came when I felt the pains. When they were getting closer together, we phoned the bush nurse, who came and sat with me, keeping me calm and timing the gaps between pains. When she thought it time, we jumped into the car (well in my case crawled, bent over and very slowly).

After travelling the winding, steep road up over the mountain range to the nearest hospital at Omeo, we arrived. The nurses put me into a wheelchair and whisked me down to my room, having told my husband he could come and see me once I was settled in. There was no such thing as hubbies being at the bedside then. After putting me into my nightie and settling me into bed, the nurse said she would go and get the equipment for the enema and shave. However, on arriving back she found, much to her surprise, that there was no time for all that. I was quickly transferred to the labour ward.

A very short time passed and my daughter was soon telling the entire world she had arrived. My astounded husband was shown in to see his daughter. He was utterly floored. He thought he was coming back to see me before I went into the labour ward. Instead I presented his daughter to him!

The whole process was very short. That is not to say I didn't have the pain, I did, and I fainted at one stage. However I was very lucky it did not drag on for ages. The result, I feel, of being a hard working farmer's wife who was used to a great deal of physical work. We were so very happy and thrilled with our new baby. Little did we know that this was the beginning of many years of sheer delight from our daughter and our sons to follow. As grandparents and other relatives gather around, I could feel the love in the room. I believe that new babies bring a great deal of love into the world when they arrive.

MY CHILDREN—MOTHER LOVE
SHARON

I stood in my bedroom looking down at the cot in which my baby daughter slept and I cried, wept heartbrokenly, sobbed and sniffed. I almost made myself sick with my intense feelings. Why? What had brought on these extremely intense emotions?

I felt so afraid, so very much in fear that I would lose this most precious jewel, the light of my life, my greatest asset. *How would I survive if I lost her? I loved her so much it literally hurt my heart.*

I stood there trying to bring myself under control and trying not to waken her. She slept on unknowing. My beautiful daughter looking so angelic with her blonde curls and her cheeks flushed with sleep, clutching her teddy in one arm and her "nighny' in the other hand, thumb in mouth. She would go nowhere without her 'nighny'. Her 'nighny' being just a cloth napkin, the corner she screwed up and played with. It was sneakily swapped for a clean one, when necessary. Something I could not do with her previous model. It began as a cot blanket very fluffy and soft. It was impossible to keep that clean, as she knew when I tried to take it from her and she would be inconsolable until it was restored to her.

It was a very gradual process weaning her from the previous one to the nappy.

The nappy was always white and I could take it to be washed and replace it with a clean one when needed. When she was tired she would put thumb in mouth, twist the corner of the 'nighny' and tickle her nose with it. It is amazing how young children get these little foibles. My youngest granddaughter has a bib as her comfort blanket, her mum having cleverly changed to the easiest item to wash and replace without her knowing.

My daughter would have been about 12-14 months old then and her 'nighny' was

still in fashion until she was about three years old. She gradually progressed from taking it everywhere to only using it when she was sleepy and then when she went to bed at night.

My little darling was a good and clever girl, wanting to help Mummy with everything. When her first baby brother arrived, she was approximately twenty three months old. She was a good little mother figure, helping with everything, and wanting to do much more than she was able.

My Darling Daughter

Daughter, Darling Daughter how the years have flown.
Once you were so tiny never to be left alone
Through the days when first you crawled, then walked
Those antics oft recalled still brings to my heart that music
That music and that heart so full already but more years go by
Showing Beauty, grace and dignity top up the heart with more.
You, when on your horses sat and trained them too
To go with you, to prance with you to show that horse and rider
Can be elegant and powerful bringing beauty
to eyes in wonder who with love and pride cannot explain
watch o'er her children and not to shirk her duty
More love adds sweetly so softly creeps in to fill some more
To that heart to my surprise, stretches gently gently to add
each day with your success which makes me proud
Your love and charm I could shout out loud
She's my daughter, darling daughter my heart still filling more
each day. My Daughter. *by Coral Boucher*

Sharon at Horse Show on her horse Silvy

THESE BOOTS

This was a story sent in to 'ABC—Moments behind the picture' and was published on computer:

"These boots are made for walking!" Looking around I saw, as expected, my darling little three year old daughter, Sharon, standing at the door wearing her yellow gumboots. Not surprising, as that little song is always the cue to announce that she is wearing them.

She starts singing "Are you ready boots? Start walking!" Off we go, singing together. With Anthony in the pram we head up to the dairy, to help milk the cows.

The last cows are coming in, as we can hear the tractor coming across the river, the shrill whistles, dogs barking, and cows mooing. A kookaburra joins in with its raucous laughter and a magpie adds its warble to lighten the chorus.

At the dairy Sharon yells "These boots are made for walking Grandpa!"

"Yes" he says, "and they had better walk on over here and do some work!"

"But Mummy said I have to stay here" she responds, standing obediently out of the way.

I shut the cow in the bail, leg rope her and call Sharon over to put the teat cups on.

She squats there, engrossed in her job, and I quickly grab the camera and take the photo.

There she is in her yellow gumboots, red tights, green corduroy skirt and dark green jumper. The white ribbon is slipping down, as usual, from her recently self-barbered hair. What a bright picture to gladden the day. Yes, those boots were made for walking and they sure do. *By Coral Boucher*

My first child, Sharon, was a real little mother's helper. She always wanted to help mummy no matter what she was doing. I have a photo of her sweeping the floor with a huge smile on her face and her 'nighnie' around her shoulders. It always makes me smile, bringing tears to my eyes. She was a very happy child who would always have a giggle about something. She was my 'medicine'. They say a laugh a day keeps the doctor away. Well she would make me laugh and thus keep the doctor away.

She was my ray of sunshine, my little mate. All my children were and are a delight to me. The eldest was the dearest little girl. She was always good natured and cheery and bright. She had very fine hair and it was very hard to groom. In the morning it would be a bird's nest at the back. I found a spray which I suppose was a spray on conditioner I was so thankful for that product. I blessed it each day. I could spray it on and brush her hair out without screams and cries. It would break my heart every time I had to brush it. I would put ribbons in her hair, but they always fell out.

One day she came out with her hair chopped off and said "It better Mummy?" I gasped and trying to hide my shock, I hugged her and said she was beautiful, but she should always let Mummy cut her hair. "I help Mummy" was her reply. Fighting back the tears I led her away and tried to make it a bit better. "Mummy's just doing a bit at the back where you couldn't reach". Some sections were almost to the scalp and others not cut at all and more cut halfway down. I tidied it up without cutting it all to the scalp and just hoped it would grow quickly. Strange but her longer hair had a flip, a pretty little curl, at the bottom, but that never appeared again.

She was absolutely besotted with horses, she just loved everything about them. She was lucky to get a half broken-in brumby. Every day she groomed her and taught her all the show horse tricks, the jumps and the fancy walking and trotting using only the slight pressure of her knees. She took part in shows and did well. I had to make her a flash mid navy jacket, and with jodhpurs and hair tied up under her helmet, a tie white shirt, she really looked the part. She made me so proud. Silver, her horse, looked the part with her main and tail plaited and all her leather gear polished to match her long boots. What a beautiful picture they made with Silver's pale grey coat shining in the sun. Unfortunately the menfolk didn't like Silver.

She was a bit of a rogue and once out of her paddock, she could make her way along the river behind the neighbours' places both up and down the river. There would often be a phone call during the day saying "Would you please shift this X*#g* horse out of our place! She's eating our something or other!"

By the time Sharon got home, the air was blue with several very weary men having tried to catch her for hours, up and down the river. The air turned even bluer when Sharon grabbed an empty bucket and the reins and walked up to the horse. "Hello Sylvie, what have you been doing today? Been a naughty girl then?"

Talking quietly, she walked slowly up to her and put the reins on, a two minute job which the men had been trying for hours to accomplish. They were not amused.

Sharon left school when she was 15. She had no interest in it and after a run in with one of the teachers, was unfairly given lower marks than was warranted and making her report card a lot worse than it should have been. She was a hard worker and was prepared to do anything within reason to earn some money.

She was waitressing at a café in Omeo and one of her next jobs was to paint the masonic hall. Then the Ensay North school and finally the Ensay football club rooms. After this life was a bit kinder to her and she became an integration aide at the Swift's Creek High School and acting secretary when the other lady was on leave.

It was about then that she went to Bairnsdale to have her Taxation form done. After seeing all the different jobs she had done, the accountant could see that she had a good work ethic. As he handed her the completed form he said laconically "Done a bit of computer work eh?"

"Oh a bit" said Sharon.

"Well would you like a job here?" He asked.

"Yes I'd love to have a job here!" which showed how smart she really was. It was only later she thought "Where will I live?" After arranging starting dates and times, salary and leave and all those necessary things, she left that office in a daze. Now it was time to work out accommodation. She had a friend sharing with another friend in Bairnsdale, and on asking if they could do with a third, she was set.

On arriving home that night, she was almost too excited to tell us. It was like a dream. She had always wanted to do accounting but that subject was not taught at Swift's Creek. I only found out many years later that she would have loved to go to boarding school and learn this subject. Even if I had known at the time, finances were far too low to even consider it. However in spite of her rough start she has done very well in spite of the setbacks and very hard work that it entailed.

She is now a fully qualified taxation accountant and with the addition of being able to audit trust Fund a Fellow. Sharon now has her own business with two or three girls working for her. Her business has grown out of sight and really needs another qualified accountant to help her.

The fact is that when she was studying at night to gain those qualifications, she worked and had two young children to look after.

TONY

Tony with Galah

Tony started life being called 'Yo-Yo'. Because It was quite a few miles to Omeo and my first baby came very quickly, I was afraid that we would leave it too late. I had a few false alarms and I was up to hospital, then back home a few times. It was on the day of his uncle's twenty first birthday and I had been taken to hospital earlier in the day. As the pains had gone again they were sending me home. His father was coming up to take me home. However when he arrived I was in labour and in a few minutes Tony was born. He surprised everyone. When Tony's father went home all the people at the party asked how things were going. He said "Nothing, another false alarm", trying desperately to keep a straight face.

J 's sister looked closely at him and he burst out laughing. They all understood then and he told them that Tony had arrived almost before his father had. So that was why Tony was nicknamed 'Yo-Yo' as he was up and down with me to hospital and back so many times.

Tony was a good and happy baby and was easy to care for. He was quite placid. As he grew we realized that he was very particular with his toys. They would remain new looking for years. Once his baby brother was old enough to share his room there was a clear demarcation line, his side and Evan's.

As they both grew older, there were many arguments about keeping to the right side of the room.

Evan liked to pull things apart to see how they worked and Ken liked to keep them as new. Woe-betide if Evan played with one of Tony's toys. The children had a little pup which they adored and when Tony was about three and the pup only tiny, he would put the pup in the back of the trike and ride him around. They both loved it.

Tony liked to help with the chores whatever it was. It was wonderful to see him and his sister helping each other with a job.

He loved to play with his cars and trucks outside. He had quite a collection. He would play in the dirt and often come in with dirt all over his face. I often asked if he had been using his nose to make roads.

I don't remember if I ever got an answer, probably just a cheeky grin.

When he was around seven or eight years old, I noticed him grunting whilst eating his meals. It seemed like he couldn't breathe through his nose. I took him to the doctor who said his adenoids and tonsils were large for some reason and he was unable to breath with his mouth closed. An operation ensued.

He needed to go to the Bairnsdale hospital and be operated on there. I will never forget seeing him just after the operation.

Perhaps I was a 'softie' but this was my little boy who was hurt. They hadn't even cleaned the blood off him.

When Tony was the correct age, he went to the kindergarten, which we had just set up in time for him to go. It was a wonderful start for the children to socialize and learn to use their hands and minds.

Cubs were the next, and then scouts and Tony loved it all. Learning to tie knots and many outdoor pursuits were his forte. He went to Perth one year and when he came home we asked how it was. "Alright" was his reply.

"What did you do?"

"Not much".

That's about all we could get out of him for a couple of days. He was probably overwhelmed by it all and had to sort out in his mind what to say first. A couple of days later he was following me around the house with "We did this Mum" and "We also did that". The words just flowed out of him and I could hardly get a word in edgeways.

He became a Queen's scout, which was a high honour in scouting. He needed to take part in many diverse difficult things. His mate Paul was awarded on the same day for the achievement.

Abseiling, caving, rock climbing, overland hiking with just a compass to guide them. Making an igloo in the snow. One major feat was a bicycle ride from Canberra, over the Snowy Mountains, back through Corryong and home. This was a very long way over steep mountains and rough and rocky tracks. It was a very trying adventure for the body.

I believe this scouting really helped Tony and gave him much more self-confidence. He was responsible for leading others through difficult and often dangerous pursuits.

He had a very good appetite, I guess because of his very physical life. I remember one day when we were just finishing our meal, a friend came in to let him know that his ride to a scout outing was waiting. I bought ice-cream in two gallon buckets those days, and the bucket being empty, he was scraping the last of it from around the sides and bottom.

His friend, with a nod of his head said "Yes, and I bet he ate the whole lot too!" Tony's appetite was well known among his friends.

Tony was a very good footballer and won several trophies for that plus running and other sports.

When he was eighteen he obtained his license. No one will ever know just how much I had to psych myself up before getting into the car whilst teaching each of my children to drive. He bought himself a small car to travel home at weekends. Unfortunately not too long after he got his car, he fell asleep on the road back to Bairsdale. It had run up a bank and flipped back on its hood. Fortunately it was not the steep banks on the earlier part of his trip, but further down near the Nicholson river. I went to pick him up to bring him home. I felt so very much for him. His first car, and he had always taken so much care of his possessions. He was gladly unhurt except for a few bruises. When we got back to Swift's Creek, I wanted to cuddle him and try to ease his pain. He said very little but wanted to be dropped off at his girlfriend's place. Ah the pain of your children growing up and away from you.

After that I worried every time one of them would be driving late at night.

When he left school he obtained an apprenticeship as a State Electricity Commission (as it was then) Linesman and did very well. He was offered a foreman's job but just preferred to work outside with the men. He didn't want to be stuck in an office if only for a few minutes.

He earned all the promotions as a live linesman and all the other steps along the way. He has always worked on call since he was given that opportunity, being called out to faults day and night for a week at a time rotating with others.

One very dangerous job was during a flood and live wires were dangling in the floodwater. Water and electricity are not a good mixture and he was up to his armpits in the water, handling live wires. I'm glad I did not know some of the dangerous jobs they would do until afterwards, as I would have been a nervous wreck. Being up at the top of an electricity pole is an everyday occurrence for him.

Tony broke his leg badly riding to work on his motorbike one very frosty morning. The lady in the car that hit him drove on to the main street and didn't see him because her windows were fogged up.

He was lucky it wasn't much worse but it caused him a lot of pain and heartache as that finished his wonderful football career. Everyone said he was most likely getting best and fairest.

He now plays tennis and joins his son playing baseball.

Tony married and bought a house in Bairnsdale and later moved to Sale and had a beautiful house built at Longford. He has four wonderful children of whom I am very proud, as I am of all my grandchildren.

I believe the stories of all my grandchildren are for another day, as I'm thinking of you dear readers who have to hold this book up to read it.

One thing I appreciate in Tony is his wit, passed down from his grandfather. You always have to watch what you say as he will always pick it up and make a wry comment about it.

Tony always seemed to know when he was needed to lighten the atmosphere if we were unhappy or such. He always has a witty remark to make us laugh. He is a wonderful man of whom I am very proud.

EVAN

Evan is the youngest of my children, who was once again a happy and placid baby and young child. His worst problem was getting into Tony's things or messing that side of the bedroom up, very reminiscent of Ken and Neil.

I am feeling the loss of a poem for the boys here. Perhaps it will come.

He also had the benefit of the kindergarten which he enjoyed very much and on Friday afternoon he went to stay with the wife of the Presbyterian minister when I went to work. I could see the benefit of this pre-schooling as my first two children did not have that benefit and I found how he was much more socialized and prepared for school when the time came.

Evan was a good sportsman and came home from school sports with lots of ribbons. He loved footy and was good at it. When the time came I decided to send Evan to boarding school. I could just afford it at the time and I realized I had to get him away from a bad situation. He did not respect his father and I was afraid for his future. With the group he associated with I thought he would be lucky to get a job at the mill.

I know he was lonely and feared he was bullied. I will always remember a little voice on the phone saying "Please let me come home Mummy".

It broke my heart and I wanted to go and bring him home at once.

I spoke to the boarding house master and he said to think very long about the reason I had sent him.

He told me not to phone for a few days. I said "I can't do that, he will think I am just ignoring him". The master said he had many years' experience and that I must trust him. It was the worst few days I had spent, worrying about him. My memory is not really clear about what happened then but I believe that he was transferred to live away from the boarding school and things seemed to settle down.

Evan was also learning to play the guitar at school.

The boys were allowed home on boarder's weekends and when he came home at end of term, I always drove to Sale to pick him up and often other boys from along our route home.

Thank goodness for the station wagon as it was stacked high with luggage. All their belongings, their sporting equipment and musical instruments came home with them at the end of term.

It was after driving from Sale and pulling into Swift's Creek, I was stopped for a breath test.

The policeman asked if I had any alcohol that day. I explained that I had driven from Swift's Creek to Sale and back again, and that I rarely had a drink. In any case, even if I did, it was just a very small glass occasionally.

I blew into the device and the policeman laughed and he said I had blown almost over the limit. We both thought it a joke when I explained that I knew that the last alcohol I had was on my daughter's friend's birthday one month ago.

It was a real laugh for the town as I was known as a virtual teetotaller. Some asked what I would have done if I had gone over the limit. I said I would have asked to go into the booze bus and have a more exact test. The policeman had just laughed and said it must have been a very good drink. As it happened it had been an expensive drop—an apricot liqueur Muscat or something like that.

After dropping all the other boys off, we were home at last after a very long day.

Unloading the car was a real chore but we soon had it done, Evan and I. After a bite to eat, we were glad to creep under our bedclothes those nights.

He really enjoyed his few days at home during holidays as he roamed the countryside and caught up with friends. The farming life was a very good life for children. They had acres to play in and spent most of their time outside. This is unlike modern youngsters who have no idea how to entertain themselves and spend little time outside.

He enjoyed practicing his guitar. It was a shame he gave it up as playing a musical instrument gives you that something extra in your life which often is lacking.

Evan seemed to settle down, doing well at his subjects. His favourite sport there was rowing at which he excelled. It's a shame he was unable to continue with it after he left school as there was no such activity to my knowledge in Bairnsdale. I found out recently that he hopped on the bus and went to Sharon's very often of a weekend. I can't understand why the school hadn't let me know as boarders were only allowed home on boarder's weekends. I'm pleased now that he was able to do this and if I had known he could actually do it, I would have arranged for him to come home more often. At least I believe he settled down because of this.

Evan, I'm proud to say, earned an apprenticeship to be a State Electricity Commission linesman with his brother. It was not a policy for them to employ brothers too often, but Evan's resume and interview earned him the place.

In approximately Evan's last year at school I moved to Bairnsdale and he was able to live with his brother and me. He was able to commence his apprenticeship in Bairnsdale. We had moved to another rental house in Bairnsdale and I had a boarder for a time.

Attached to the garage was a room which we cleaned and painted out. The landlord had agreed to supply the paint if we painted it. I put up curtains and was able to get a remnant piece of carpet from a cousin who worked in a carpet factory.

With a bed in there and it having plenty of cupboard space, the room was quite cosy. I had a boarder in there for a while until he finished his schooling, when he moved back to his parent's home in Lakes Entrance. His few dollars brought in much needed money. He was a nice young fellow and no trouble at all and fitted in well with the way the home was run.

I cooked his meal at night and breakfast was a quick and easy cereal. I cut sandwiches for his lunch and he went home at the weekend, taking his washing with him.

When the boarder left, Evan moved into the bungalow and it suited him well. He had a degree of independence. He met a young girl and they eventually became an item. Evan later moved out to live at his girlfriend's place.

Evan, I'm sorry to say almost mimicked his brother in that he crashed his car just after getting it. He had a finger stitched. They say that the ring anaesthetic on a finger is one of the most painful, because of the many needles needed around a delicate finger. He was fortunately not hurt any more than that. One of his mates travelling with him got a broken leg. This mate was very emphatic that it had not been Evan's fault. It seems a four wheel drive was travelling very fast coming from the other direction and forced Evan into the rough edge of the road. His car hit a tree. Fortunately he was not driving too fast.

The worst part about it was that he was just going to have it insured the next day when he got paid. I didn't know this at the time as he was living at his girlfriend's place, or I might have been able to help him with the insurance money.

The car was a write-off and Evan decided to break the car down and sell it bit by bit. He believed he would get more for it than selling it to a wrecker. Luckily ours was a double garage and he was able to store it and work on it there.

Now, the tragic thing was that he had to save up again before he could buy another. I was having a battle financially so was unable to help him out.

Another time, Evan was driving me home from Traralgon. It may have been whilst he was still on Learner's Plates. We were travelling with the sun warm, coming through the window. I had probably run out of things to talk about, as was my want, and the car started drifting to the other side of the road. A car behind us gave a toot and I looked at Evan. He was dozing off.

I yelled "Evan!" and grabbed the wheel. He looked up and immediately corrected his path as a car was coming from the other direction, wanting his share of the road.

This was another reason why I worried about them driving especially late at night, on their own, although this was during the day.

He continued going with his girlfriend for quite a few years then they decided to marry. I was thrilled. She was a lovely girl. I loved her dearly. My mother also loved her and admired her for the way she kept the house and eventually the children.

I'm afraid I spoiled their wedding as I had a bad cough at the time and, not wanting to miss seeing them married, I stayed in the church longer than I should have. I would have spoiled it all with my constant coughing. I eventually crept out of a side door and a man brought me a glass of water. I was able to join them for photos. There has never been anything said to me, but I'm sure it was the case. Another thing I'm extremely sorry for.

They were forced to cut their honeymoon short, I believe because they had assumed I could help them with more money than I actually could. I have not been told this but somehow I have got this impression in the time since. I am extremely sorry for this. I was working part time and paying the rent on my own by then and I just could not save any more. It had not occurred to me to borrow money for this as this was not my normal way. Maybe I have it all wrong, but I now regretfully believe it to be so.

They had a very heart breaking time for some years after deciding to have children and then desperately wanting them. They tried and tried and still remained childless until, at last they came to me with the best news. They were expecting. What joy. We were all so happy for them and couldn't wait to see the new family member. At last a beautiful little boy arrived

Two little girls arrived then in the next few years, a very beautiful family

Evan moved up in his work gaining promotion by attending courses and gaining qualifications.

When the time came for Evan to gain promotion to higher duties, he moved into the office and rarely joined the work gangs. He also took the on the on-call duty and has done to this day. He worked many extra hours and added to his family's coffer. They would often be called out at night and often a few times a night. Evan and his brother often missed out on family times at Christmas and other holidays and children's birthdays. I remain very proud of them both for sacrificing sleep and those special times for the sake of their families.

Evan continued to rise in his job and was eventually became his elder brother's boss. Tony had no worries with this as he had always said he wanted to stay on the gang with the boys. Evan became district manager and organized the gangs to go to each job. I'm very, very proud of him. He is a very deep man. A man who feels deeply when many would not know it. He is a quiet, wonderful man, very caring and loving.

He now plays tennis, evening golf and joins his son at soccer, taking the role of running the boundary.

The poem I wished to write for my boys has surfaced. Not two separate ones but for both combined:

Tony, Evan, Sharon

THAT'S THE WAY
THEY LIKED IT

My boys, my boys, my dearest boys,
With snowy hair and noisy toys.
Helped all they could with vigour
'Cos work on the farm there always was
for smaller and for bigger
So long as Mum cooked up a feed,
they'd eat it all with greed.
Then when the creek was flowing fast
down they'd go and float a raft.
If danger there was to them then
that's the way they liked it
In dirt they'd play
They'd stay out all day
And the dirtier they got the better
For that's the way they liked it.
Muddy football boots, socks and shorts.
after a tough and scrambling game
that's the way they liked it.
Then kindness and thought
for others for nought.
Once on a job they'd never shirk
Work on they did for they were committed
do anything at all if they were permitted.
So proud I am of both my boys
Grown to manhood now and with cheeky grins
and prickly chins

they keep us all delighted
Great fathers they are to children taught
to respect their elders as they ought
Adored by their children, each other, sister and I
They will give anything a try
Good with their hands they fix and make,
machinery and timber, a fence or gate.
As you can tell by now, as my verse is done
I love those boys each as one. *By Coral Boucher*

I often said to one or all my children, "If you don't behave yourselves I'll give you a clip 'side the ear", meaning a slap beside the ear, something I never did. The result was that every time I said it they would all burst into gales of laughter. I therefore often said it just to make them laugh. Not a very good disciplinary action, but sometimes they forgot about being naughty in their laughter.

A very joy to the ears is a child's laughter.

KINDERGARTEN

Several of us mothers set up a Pre-School centre. We formed it in spite of all the red tape involved with all the government departments. We paid the teacher and assistant with funds paid for fees. We bought all the necessary equipment—all specially designed with pre-school children in mind.

Fortunately the teacher had previous experience and knew what was required. This was in 1974 and Topsy Newcomen is still the teacher, to my knowledge to this day. I took on the role of treasurer as I had experience in handling money. When you handle so much each day at a bank, you don't think of it as money, just paper.

Because of this fear from others of handling money, I stayed as Treasurer from its inception for ten years. The other office bearers changed every so often as was the rule.

The Pre-school centre eventually became a kindergarten and the teacher's salary was paid by the Omeo Shire.

Life went on with things getting tougher on the farm with devastating droughts year after year. At least one year the river stopped running and there were just the odd deep pools. It was very difficult trying to keep the stock alive. It was heart breaking seeing them so thin with all ribs and backbones showing.

Paid Work

When we first married my husband said to me, "You will not work. No wife of mine will ever work".

However, with droughts years after year, the farm was still keeping us all busy but was making no money. My husband would work all hours, cutting, raking and baling hay.

We would all put our time in at the dairy each day, even J's mother. I would bake bread till late at night making enough for the childrens' lunches and breakfast toast etc. so needed about eight loaves per week. I made butter for us and to sell. I sold plants in pots and worked hard. I made the childrens' clothes and the vegetables from my garden kept food on the table.

One day I was offered a job. My youngest child was going to kindergarten now and we badly needed the money. The job was at the post office on the manual telephone exchange. I decided to take it and though my husband was not happy about it, he had to agree.

I arranged for a lady to look after E after kindergarten on Friday as the job was for that day plus Saturday and Sunday afternoons and until ten o'clock Sunday night.

Because it was shift work and covered the weekends, I received good wages. I was not apart from the children when they were at home. J was able to give them a meal on Sunday night.

I still did my shift at the dairy on Friday morning before going to work.

Manual Telephone Exchange

Once I had learned the work on the exchange, I enjoyed it.

When it got really busy I revelled in the challenge. I prided myself in switching very quickly for the local calls. I had to dial up a trunk call but not a local call, as the home numbers did not have that facility. When very busy I would have call dockets for trunk calls, increasing by the minute. We had six trunk lines which carried incoming calls as well as those outgoing. If a number was busy for a trunk call, I would tell the caller it was engaged and I would call them back. Some days and at certain times one number was needed by a lot of men. It was to the T.A.B. in Bairnsdale and race days it would be very hard to get through. We all grew to remember a popular trunk line number, say to the doctor's clinics in Bairnsdale, to Foards or Dahlsens.

The local numbers were quickly remembered but it was not really a necessity, as most people would ask for the number. Some people were too busy or too whatever to look up a number in the book, and would just ask for "*So and So's place*" or the local store or butcher.

I guess some did not have long enough arms to read the fairly small print in the phone book.

To raise us at the exchange, local callers needed to twirl a handle on the old phones.

As the customer asked for a local number, a little shutter would drop down and a low buzz was given. We would then plug the end of a cord into the asking number and the other end was plugged into the required number. After plugging in, we pulled back a little joystick which would make the phone ring at the required number. When the call was finished the customers were required to give a little ring to let us know that the call was over.

If someone else wanted one of the two numbers, we would tell the caller we would phone them back when the line was free.

Sometimes people would chat for hours and the second caller would ring us, thinking we had forgotten them. If one of the callers had forgotten to ring off, we would not know if the line was free. Sometimes we had to go across the line to hear if they were still talking.

However, this would not always work as, thinking we were listening to them, they would stop talking. We would then need to say "Are you free?" or some such words. I was never guilty of eavesdropping, but had inadvertently caught a word or two when doing my job. Sometimes someone would not hear the click as we went across the line and keep talking. In any case, anything heard there was kept strictly in confidence.

I had never been a gossip and try never to be caught in this respect, then or now.

I knew what damage gossiping could do, especially when passed on incorrectly or even if true it is no-one else's business but their own. Nevertheless I do believe one girl was often said to listen in on conversations.

For the busiest times, like Christmas, Mothers' and Fathers' day, we would have two girls on the exchange. The switchboard could be pulled apart to make two separate ones.

We would both be very busy at those times. I would love it as I loved the very busy times on my own. On would go the headsets, the sleeves pulled up, and both hands going like a thrashing machine.

The times when the switchboard was quiet, when the post office was open, I would help sort the mail. The switchboard had first call on me, but I enjoyed helping out.

On Sunday night and Saturday afternoon, the switchboard was a bit quieter and we could catch up with knitting and reading. This was allowed so long as the switchboard was not neglected. I did a lot of knitting in those days, knitting jumpers for the children and my hubby. I did a few for myself but was never really happy with them.

The children would snuggle into the thick woollies in the cold. There were not really items around like fleece tops or trousers then. When the children were little, on a cold and dreary day with no gardening to be done, the children napping, I could sit, feet in the warming oven of the slow combustion stove. I would knit away and read at the same time and finish a jumper in a day. I would cast on the stitches late morning and be sewing the pieces together that night. Thank goodness for that twelve ply wool. It was a good feeling to have achieved something as the jumpers were needed in our climate.

I think I only managed that once or twice as there was always baking or butter making and dressmaking and house work to keep me busy. I remember once when, after a fall of snow, I was out at the clothesline. There were always nappies to be washed in those days, no expensive artificial ones for my children. Clad in gum boots, woolly hat and drab old coat, city visitors pulled up. I'm sure they would never be seen in such old unfashionable clobber. I wished the snow had been deeper and I could sink right in!

POST OFFICE

When the switchboard was quiet, and having got the hang of the letter sorting, I gradually learnt more and more of the post office work.

I already knew the banking with the Commonwealth Savings Bank agency being there as in most post offices those days. Having worked in a bank before marriage, I only needed to brush up on the differing doings of the other bank. Each Friday I would learn a little more and sometimes I would fill in on the switchboard when one of the other girls went on leave, so I had a few more days during the week to help with the post office work. After a while, I was given permission to act as postmistress when the postmaster and his wife went away on holidays.

I would move into the house attached to the post office as the switchboard was manned twenty-four hours a day. The children were older by then and J could look after them when I was at work.

The night alarm was set, being a louder one to wake you from sleep. There were not that many calls during the night. They were mainly emergencies. I didn't take long to get used to them. However it was suggested we train J for the switchboard so he could give me a break at night.

After a while J was ready to take a shift on the exchange while I was acting P.M. We would all move down to the P.O. house for the usual two weeks each year.

Then when it was time for them to return, we all had to pack up and go home and I would rush around tidying the house. We all kept it fairly clean, but children don't always do what you would want them to. Mrs P.M. was a very neat lady and kept the house beautifully.

DREAMS

It was a couple of years after J had been doing the odd shift on the switch when our dream to own a post office ourselves raised its head. The Postmaster and his wife were always looking out for another post office in another area.

If they had gone ahead, we may have been able to buy the post office. It would need to be an unofficial post office with manual switch as these where were the good money was.

The Postmaster would own the house with the Australia Post paying rent on the room where the post office and switch was carried out. The Postmaster and his wife were both paid by Australia Post for the work they did. The extra two people required to run the switchboard were also paid by Australia Post. Some of the exchanges were going automatic, as Swift's Creek was about to.

We found a good post office in Southwest Victoria, which were a few years away from going automatic. It was a good price and we would have been gone from there except the other part owners of the farm would not sell up or buy us out. Without their cooperation, we could not do it. I think this may have been when and why J's condition started.

Fortunately finances were better for us as J got a job on the Lands Dept. and he was bringing in a good wage. Probably the first real paying job he had. He had worked for years on the farm and got little or nothing. We had been living on my part time income. That farm was not a good proposition. It was a dairy farm in a non-dairy area. The droughts had been the last blow. All of us, even J's mother, put in some time at the dairy along with our other chores. If a time and motion study had been done it would have been ludicrous. All working our insides out for a few miserable dollars a month. Not enough to feed the chooks let alone three families.

The exchange went automatic and we were all made redundant.

I was still getting work as acting P.M. once a year.

FLABBERGASTED

One day, when I was shopping at the store, the owner's wife came up to me. She said her husband wanted to talk to me.

On going into the house with them I was offered a job.

They asked if I wanted a job and I said we didn't really need for me to work now, but I agreed as I was ready for another challenge.

On the day they asked me to work for them and although I didn't need to, I was looking to the future and selling myself to them. I had only just been asked to work for them ten minutes ago, I had not any time to think it over but I was telling them that I could learn the work and take over as acting manager when they went on holidays. I certainly had belief in myself then.

They must have been flabbergasted, but I could see another challenge. I already knew the banking agency, so I could do that straight away, and within a short time my boast came to fruition. Whilst I was basically shy, I had confidence in my ability. There was a lot to learn, from using the till to pricing up items and stacking shelves.

Days when I was there alone and someone would want a dozen cold beers from the cool room, I literally ran up that ramp and back down with the trolley. When the shop was empty I'd dash up to the cool-room again to get more cabbages and lettuce. I dread to think what items were shoplifted when we were on our own in the shop.

If one was on the till and someone had pulled a price sticker off, I had to go and check the price on the shelf. I knew what the shoplifters were doing, but what could I do?

I took over the paper returns and did them each month. Then the liquor department became my area with the ordering and stocking up.

We had a man come into the shop who spoke through a hole in his throat. He spoke in huffs of air through this hole. He always asked for me, because I was the only one who could understand him.

Two other old men would ask for me or wait until I was free, as I always had the patience to help them with their order.

We had a new computerised till delivered and I was taken in to the house to learn it.

With the new till, you keyed all the prices in and for those people who had accounts, it printed on a card the transaction and showed the balance owing. Some days you would get the lot. Someone wanting to pay some cash on some things and wanting to pay a cheque off the account. Pay days at the mill were very busy as a large percentage of the mill workers had accounts.

The new till was great fun. I had to teach the other girls how to use it, so I had to stand behind them and tell them what to do for a few weeks. The boss said I wasn't making enough mistakes. He thought you needed to learn by your mistakes.

Then I was put in charge of the microfiche machine to look up prices etc.

The store was given a major overhaul, with new freezers and fridges. There was some shelving in the newsagency area for something else. The boss asked me what I thought would sell well for there. He left me to order, unpack and arrange it all. I thought that little cheap earrings and jewellery would sell as there was nothing else in this town The nearest big enough town was Bairnsdale which was some sixty miles away.

I bought in a lot of such things and cheap gift items. I also bought in some kitchen gadgets. I'm pleased to say they all sold like hot cakes. I couldn't keep up with them. The young girls bought a lot and even the older ladies bought some. The little plastic earrings were cute and I bought a couple of pairs to match what I wore to work.

I gradually took over the ordering for the frozen goods, and the dairy products.

So it happened that I was doing all the ordering for the shop with no input from the boss.

And so it came to pass as they say, and I did take over as acting manager. I'm not sure how much time had elapsed since I had made that rash promise, but it happened.

I did not work full time except for when the bosses were away. I was kept busy on the farm as well as with this exciting work.

TELEVISION OFF

When the children became a bit older and able to play table games, the television was switched off every Saturday night. Saturday night was family night and the television was not turned on no matter what was on. I'm sure we all benefitted from this. There were card games and board games and depending whether we started early or late which game we would play. Monopoly was a favourite if we started early. The same applied to Stock Market.

There was another long game too but I can't recall its name. There was also Headache and Pop-ups and many others. It taught the children how to count and handle money and even helped with languages. I would talk the little I could remember in French, the numbers and a few other things and, my daughter would often relate that to the German she was learning. It also taught them to play together with no fights. I believe we all enjoyed those nights.

The Most Horrific Venture

The road from Swift's Creek to Bairnsdale was a nightmare to drive at the best of times

One day we set off, the three children safely strapped into the back seat of the station wagon. They were all very excited as it was a treat to spend a day in Bairnsdale, with so many shops and much more to see. It was early in the morning as it was a full day to drive there, do what was needed and then drive back again. There was a bit of "Mummy where are my socks?" "Mummy, can I take my truck?" "Mummy, what will I wear?" "Mummy what will we eat?"

At last we set off, grateful for the heater in the car as it was very frosty outside. We had had a lot of rain in the last few days, but today, thankfully, it was clear and bright.

The road was very windy, following the river at the bottom of the valley. We came upon a few rocks across the road which I had to dodge and at each corner it was a certainty that a car would come around the corner on our side at one or the next

There were no white lines and people didn't pay any attention to the arrow and speed signs.

One day whilst travelling with my city cousin in his M G. I had a very hairy ride. He scoffed at the speed marked as the safest to negotiate that particular bend. He soon found out his mistake as, attempting to round it at his speed, he was forced with a squeal of his brakes and a fight with the steering wheel, to stay on the road. After a couple more such instances, he settled down and obeyed the signs. His bone-white complexion slowly returned to its natural hue. City drivers have no concept of the sharpness of those bends allied with the width of the road.

To return to our present day excursion—I rounded one corner to see a huge log truck looming toward us on my side of the road. "Ooh Mummy!" came from the back "Look Out!" I was able to slow to a stop, slightly scraping the bank on our side and halted. The truck slowly inched past. The corners were too sharp and the road too narrow for a truck to round those corners without using the whole width of the road. Trucks just did not bend in the middle.

We continued on with the trio in the back a bit quiet from their shock, passing all the roadside names well known to travellers on that road. Plucking up their nerve they were fighting over who had guessed the correct name first. The 'Snakes Back' and 'Haunted Stream' only two of the many who have been itemized by other authors in previous novels.

After another straight stretch, there was again much chattering from the back-seat drivers. They all had marvellous ideas about how it would have been better to cope with that truck and what I should do next. The next hazard was a great fall of rock across the road. With the banks so steep and no slope away at the top (as modern roads have) after a good fall of rain loosens the soil around the trees and rocks then down they would slide. I braked sharply accompanied by many "Oh Mummy!", "Help", "Sit down" and "What will you do?"

After surveying the situation, I saw that if I could roll a fair sized rock and then another out of the way, we might make it. Regrettably I needed the children to help as the thought of walking Bairnsdale with a filthy crew did not appeal. "Well mates are you ready to help?"

"Can I drive the car?"

"What can I do?"

"Am I too little?"

I explained how they could help and with the least mess to their clothes. We pulled and tugged, tugged and pulled, with most of the time all of us pulling together.

At last the larger boulders were out of the way and we could inch through. I was thinking to myself, *"I hope someone comes and cleans this off before we come back later"*.

After travelling along peacefully for some time, enjoying the bird calls and the aroma of the bush, we rounded a corner and suddenly . . . .

The car took on a mind of its own, no matter what I did. I was unable to regain control of the car. I tugged at the wheel, pulled on the handbrake, the car just went its merry way. If I had read Harry Potter or some such book I would be thinking that aliens had taken over. The screams from the backseat were deafening. The car headed towards the high cliff, just scraping the sides, then zigged to the left and zagged to the right. What was happening? Then it was heading for the other bank, the one where the river ran some feet below. "Oh no!" We were all terrified that we would be over the bank and into the water.

This all happened very quickly and in no time the car was teetering over the edge of the cliff towards the water. "Mummy, Mummy what can we do?"

"Just don't move an inch," I replied, "Its. . . . . Whoa it's slipping!"

With that the car slipped further over the edge. Too petrified to move, we sat like statues. However children can never sit like statues for long and the youngest was crying and trying to be comforted by his big sister. The older boy was trying to be brave but could not come up with any good ideas. I thought the children may be able to slip over the back seat into the luggage area, but one tiny movement would have the car groaning and threatening to slip further. Whilst we all sat there in terror, thinking of all the worst things which could happen, we heard something, very faint at first then growing louder. Was it our saviour or was it something which could not help? Then the noise grew louder and it sounded like a 4x4 ute. It rounded the corner and that was when we started to yell as the car reminded us of our precarious position.

"Well, well! What have we here eh?" said a deep voice of one of the Forest Commission men. "In a bit of a pickle, eh?"

"Yes", I whispered, thinking my voice would cause our car to move a little further.

"Well she's just caught on a big rock there, just teetering though. Could go at any time. Better move yourselves or you'll all end up in the drink. Now don't move till I say".

"Bert, better hook the winch onto the towbar of the car then the kids can climb over the back here".

As the winch was hooked on and the slack taken up, the car groaned and shimmied and shook. I did the same with my heart in my mouth. Then Jack said, "Climb over here now kids. I'll get the back open". Once the kids were out standing shakily on the road, Jack said "Right now! You Mum, over you come". I scrambled quickly to safety, for once not thinking of being ladylike. I just needed to be there with my kids. I stepped out onto the road, my feet shaking and hugged my babies to me. We were safe!

With the winch hooked on to the back of the car, the rescue mission began. Slowly, slowly the car moved back onto the road. There they were the ute, butting against the high cliff, the tow rope stretched tautly to the car and all I could think of was another car careering around the corner into them all.

After parking the car safely on the side of the road, Bob got out and said, "Well there yer are then. Safe and sound! Now just sit quietly there for a while to settle the old nerves and yer'l be right as rain". With hardly time for me to thank them, they were off, maybe to rescue another damsel in distress.

We sat for a while with the children chattering their shock away, then got out and looked at the patch of black ice and at the rock which had saved us from plunging into the river. We walked around a bit and then we got back in and resumed our journey.

Black ice is formed in a sheltered spot, usually a concave corner on a tarred road after a very heavy frost. It can't be seen by the driver and is very treacherous.

Continuing on our way, with the children regaining their high spirits, they played I-Spy and all those car games still played by most children on a long journey. However, one game unique to the Omeo Highway was, *'Who would be the first to see the old man'* of which I have spoken before. It is greatly changed now since then, but still a part of that special game played by children as they travel that valley road.

Another time on a trip we had a confrontation with a wombat. Very often the wombat is killed but not before rendering the car un-driveable. At least without some tugging and pulling at bent mudguards or bumper bar. Wallabies and kangaroos can often come to a quick end on that road, some doing quite an amount of damage to a car. One lady was shocked one day by a kangaroo jumping from the high bank down onto the bonnet of the car. Luckily the kangaroo lived to fight another day.

We often saw many such sad sights as these animals lying beside the road with their toes in the air. Especially during a dry season, the animals will head for the river to drink, and because of the sharp bends, particularly at night, it is very hard to see them until too late.

We continued our trip without further such excitement, the children having a very shocking story to tell at school.

At least once I was forced to change a tyre, but on another day, I had the spare wheel out, the jack and jack handle, but there was no wheel spanner. I could do nothing but wait for an infrequent vehicle to come along. I was then given a bit of cheek about helpless ladies until they saw my problem. I asked the man to demonstrate how to change a wheel without a spanner. He grinned wryly and went quickly to his vehicle to get the required tool with little else to say.

SHEARING

After I was married I helped in the shearing—shed and did my share of meals and cooking and sandwiches.

I would also usually help with the roustabout.

We had our own shearing shed then and so after putting some time in at the dairy, I would usually run back to bring 'smoko' to the shed.

At one stage when my children were in school, my mother in law was ill and unable to take part in any of the shearing work so it was up to me to do the lot.

After milking in the morning, I would give the children their breakfast and get them off to school. I would then race down to the shop to get fresh bread and cold meat or something for the sandwiches. I'd make the sandwiches and take the morning 'smoko' to the shed. I would work there for an hour or so, then race home to get the lunch ready and on the table as the men walked in.

At that time, we had two stands and my husband shore at one and we hired a shearer for the other.

J's father would do a bit at the shed and his brother would be involved with penning up and moving the sheep around and keeping strict count of the sheep before they were let out of each receiving pen.

The tar pot was another job he had to do. If a sheep had a cut where the blades had nicked it, a daub of tar was the best thing to prevent infection and fly strikes.

'R' would arrange his time to take over in the shed when I had the food to prepare.

Hands got a very good scrub up between jobs, but I didn't have time to change.

A pinny went on over my shed clothes whilst preparing and serving the food. Unfortunately the pinny didn't cover the sheep smell but I guess we all emitted that distinctive fragrance so it would not be noticed.

Luckily it was summer and we had plenty of veggies in the garden and the men liked salad, so long as it was accompanied by hot potato and peas and good solid lumps of meat.

We killed our own beasts usually, to keep us in meat so I would cook up a corned beef or pumped leg at night so we could have it for lunch the next day.

The men looked for dessert for lunch too so, luckily, we had fresh stewed fruit from our orchard or some previously preserved with freshly made custard and good rich cream to top them.

The evening meal for the family was a rushed affair after me helping in the dairy. It would probably be salad again, as the nights would see me cooking cakes and biscuits for the smokos. The children's' cooked vegetables could wait another day. As the men always enjoyed a good slab of fruit cake, I had previously baked a couple of my boiled fruit cakes, so that saved me a bit of time.

Needless to say I was very pleased when those particular shearing days ended. I was also thankful that I didn't have to do the lot each year.

I learned to do all the jobs in the shearing shed, all except the actual shearing! I would not even attempt that as I knew I would be roped into doing it all the time.

My husband went out shearing for a while with other shearing teams and he quite enjoyed it. The biggest trouble then was, other than his back, the thistles in his hands and even in his legs. He wore the correct trousers for shearing with double layers on the legs, where needed, and also the shearers flannel shirt with double layers at the ribs, but they did not help much.

The thistles would stick into his hands, legs and ribs and would become infected.

We would be digging thistles out and applying antiseptic at night during the shearing season. I made him a pair of canvas chaps and a leather apron which helped a bit.

This was why the first thing the shearer looked at was if there were many thistles in the wool. It was not only the shearer who got the thistles it was everyone else handling the wool in the shed. Even just picking up the fleece and throwing it (correctly, I might add!) There was a special way to bundle up the fleece, pick it up and throw it to cover the table neatly.

Once you had been shown a time or two, it was a terrible sin to throw it incorrectly. If not thrown in the correct manner, the person, often the rouser, skirting the fleece would take a lot longer. It also made it much more difficult to sort the good fleece from the bad. It could result in having to bundle up the fleece and throw it again. This would often result in the fleece falling apart.

This would hold up the whole shed as there was only one fleece table. A fleece once thrown was 'skirted' by pulling the leg wool and the 'daggy' bits off and then put into the pieces bin.

The good fleece was rolled correctly and put into its bin. If the fleece fell apart, it would need to be put into the pieces bin. The pieces wool was inferior, not bailed with the good fleeces and fetched a lower price.

Even though the shearer was treated as a king they were often rough, rude and would swear like a trouper. I guess they thought that if a woman was doing a man's work in a shed they should be able to take what came. However, I did admire them for doing a backbreaking and stinking hot job, with rarely a break. I don't remember seeing a shearer with any fat on him. They all looked very fit, and even graceful, as their hands flowed down over the sheep's back, almost like a dance step as they changed position to turn the sheep over, their leg going out and then under the sheep's back.

I could see the strain on their faces as they gritted their teeth and stood to drag yet another woolly out and I imagined him thinking, *"Another one and how many more?"* Probably he was just concentrating on his job and thinking how he could beat him this time.

Some shearers chased the shearing all over Victoria and even into New South during the season. My husband did this for a while to put food on our plates.

HAY CARTING

The menfolk took on contract hay carting so summer was always busy with the Lucerne.

Mowing, raking, baling and carting the bales to the hayshed, our own Lucerne kept them busy as hay making is ordered by the weather.

The Lucerne must be cut when it was ready. It was then raked at the correct time, allowing the hay to dry out a bit before it was touched again, Hay too green would heat up in the shed and could spontaneously combust. Hay too dry would lose all its leaves and have only stem to bale up. So it was often late at night, maybe eleven or twelve o'clock when J would head out to bale the hay.

I would often be called upon to drive the truck for both our own hay and for the contract carting. This would involve driving the truck and steering close enough so that the bales could be nudged onto the loader.

Once the loader had the bale onto the truck, the men would stack it neatly to make sure they could get the maximum number on and so that none fell off on the trip to the hayshed.

When we carted out at Bindi, the lady of the house would have a much needed cuppa for us after we had finished putting the hay in the shed.

There were usually sandwiches or scones and cakes to accompany it. All I would be interested in was a good cup of tea. I had been up on the truck moving bales around too so I was hot and dusty as well as the men. Some people are amazed at us drinking hot tea and think that it would be too hot. A lovely cup of tea is a great thirst quencher.

GINGER BEER

A very popular drink when we were young was Ginger Beer. One reason was that it was non-alcoholic, and another that is was very cheap to make.

We all gathered up bottles and cleaned them up. We needed to start with a starter which was some ginger paste left from a previous batch or borrow one from a neighbour.

An amount of the starter was put into a bowl with sugar and lemon juice. It was left to cure for a time then water was added and a light liquid ensued. As each bottle was filled with this mixture, a small amount of sugar was added before sealing the bottles.

Apparently it was never found what the exact ratio of sugar to liquid, because a very large percentage of the bottles tried to imitate Vesuvius. We could be sitting quietly, or hard at work in the garden, or even in bed when an enormous explosion would bring us to our feet. The first time we heard it, it was "What the heck's that?" Then came another such explosion. Did anyone know? Was it a gun or a bomb? What? Living peacefully in the country we had heard rifle fire at foxes etc. and shotgun fire.

But this was different. Had someone set off a bomb? Creeping slowly around the house, we gradually homed in on the tank stand. Creeping towards it, we were stopped dead by another louder one. What Is It? The glass flying enforced Dad and Uncle's suspicion. Yes they thought, looking towards each other with eyebrows raised. Bang! Bang! There were more now and only the brave stayed to see the outcome.

"No I wouldn't go in there Ken, Jim. It's too dangerous!" 'What could be dangerous there thought the tough teenagers. There's only a few . . . *POING!* Glass ricochets off something. We had our answer! The bottles were exploding and shooting glass everywhere. Now we knew what it was. It wasn't so dangerous we thought, then *BANG! POING! CLINK!* We raced for our lives! We were all prepared to take the advice of the adults. We left it all alone. The explosions continued spasmodically over the next few days. Rather like corn popping. How could there be anything left to drink?

At last it was deemed safe to go in. Bedlam! Disaster! What a waste. Some mourned the drink we could have had, others saw the mess and thought how much work it would take to clean up and others thought of the waste of good sugar and ginger.

Another popular drink made in a similar way was 'Pink Champagne' made with rhubarb. It was considered a more superior drink if you managed to save a couple of bottles.

My Aunt made a batch and put it into 2 litre sherry bottles and stored them under the trough in the laundry. The resultant explosion blew the front off the cupboard and glass was everywhere.

Perhaps someone managed to get the mixture right eventually, but I do know that many, many attempts were made with little success. Anyone who tasted the smallest sip, made it their business to tend the rhubarb with plenty of cow manure and plenty of water.

The long dark stems are delicious. I have never met anyone who liked it raw or cooked without sugar, but with sugar and baked in a pie with apple it was a sheer delight. Rhubarb stewed with a fair amount of sugar on breakfast cereal was a great favourite and rhubarb and apple crumble was a delectable desert.

Luckily there was plenty of rhubarb in the garden and apples on our trees.

HOUSE PAINTING

As the years went by, I painted each room one at a time. The bathroom, which was quite a large room for a bathroom. The lounge room which I considered an important one as we had friends around often. The kitchen and our bedroom were painted before we moved in. I painted the two children's rooms and took a lot of trouble with giving the old doors an antique look along with the skirting boards and architrave.

I was able to get offcuts of carpet for the two rooms from a cousin who worked in a carpet factory in Geelong.

I enjoyed doing that. Another reason for having the lounge room painted, was that J 's sister was getting married and we agreed to have the reception at our place in the lounge. There were not a lot of guests, but we took all the furniture out and put in a long trestle table or two and put white sheets on them.

I did flower arrangements for the tables and made Judy's dress. It must have been fairly simple although I remember appliqueing edges of lace to the sleeves. I also made Burgundy coloured wide whale corduroy jeans for the two little boys, Tony and Robbie, who were around the same age. I made bow ties and we had a bit of a panic to find plain white shirts for them. We must have found them. Did I also make the flower girls dresses? I'm not sure now. The wedding and reception all went off very well and we all managed to fit into our lounge.

Quite some time later I painted the outside of the house with the help of a good friend. We would pull the truck in beside the house, put two forty-four gallon drums on the back and a long solid plank across the drums. As the house was over a hundred years old and maybe had never any paint on it, the knot holes were falling out and the boards were very rough. Because of the condition of the timber, we decided to use fence type paint. One used by the Forest Commission for their signs. We were able to buy it a bit cheaper. This paint had the advantage of not showing up the roughness of the boards and could be painted straight onto them.

I'm very grateful to my friend for helping me. We did work like a barter system. He helped me with the painting of my house and I helped him making cement bricks and putting up shingles on the holidays units' walls.

There should be more of this type of thing, helping each other with a big (or little) job. That way a job gets done where it may have not been done without this help. These very good friends kept me sane and alive during my very bad times. Bless them, dearest friends.

HIT AND GIGGLE

One day another very good friend of mine called Liz asked me in the shop where I was working at that time, if I would go for a game of golf each week on our day off. I agreed and we had a wonderful time. On a Wednesdays there were probably no other golfers around and we played at our own pace. The golf course was beautiful, surrounded by pine trees and usually beautifully green. The air was fresh and it was so peaceful, with maybe the odd note of birdsong.

We loved our day out, away from the hassles of everyday life. I had never played golf before and I'm not sure if Liz had. It didn't matter if we took a long time to play a hole or went through it quickly. If we wanted to have a sit down half way through a hole it didn't matter. We usually stopped at a particular spot to have our tetra packs of juice. Sometimes we played well and this gave us the incentive to go back and surely play better at more holes than before. One of the biggest challenges was to get it over the creek. Usually we would hit a ball that far easily, but, because the water was there, we usually end up in it! We spent a lot of time looking for balls. I don't know why we gave it up. Perhaps it was winter and we didn't go out in winter. I'm sorry, for whatever reason our wonderful days stopped.

Maybe that's when about when I moved to Bairnsdale. My memory evades me but I hope I came and told you that I was going. If not I'm very very sorry and my only excuse was that I was very stressed out at that time and not thinking too well. I still hold dear your friendship and our days out together.

COINCIDENCE?

Things were becoming unbearable at home and I had been praying for I long time for someone, somehow to get me out of there. You didn't get any assistance in those days. I had no m0ney, no home and no job. I felt I was stuck there.

However my guardian angel had been watching over me and the most amazing thing happened.

They say that God never gives you anything you can't handle, but I had had my doubts for many years.

I was at work at the supermarket one day when my boss called me into the room at the back. *"What have I done now?"* I thought. I didn't really think I had done anything wrong as I worked my hardest and did my best at that job, as I had done with all of the others. However, instead of chastising me, he offered me a job. In Bairnsdale!

My boss and his wife and family were moving to Bairnsdale to combine with a friend in another business there and the supermarket was to be sold.

I was told later that W had said to his wife, "I wish we had Coral to work for us down there?"

Her answer was "Well why not ask her?"

"Oh she wouldn't want to move to Bairnsdale would she?"

L, knowing more of my situation than he did said, "Just ask her".

Well I burst into tears and could have kissed them both right there and then, and as it turned out, it was the exact time when it would work. Sharon had been offered a promotion and was moving to Sale and Tony was looking for someone to share the house and rent as Sharon and Tony had been sharing a house. It was meant to be.

My Guardian Angels had been listening after all.

Evan would be able to come back to Bairnsdale and live with us and wouldn't need to board. This was much better on my pocket, but his father did help out with school fees until he left school.

So I moved to Bairnsdale to live with my boys and began another chapter in my life of challenges.

ACCOUNTS LADY

As it turned out the house they were renting was at the back of my new workplace.

I was shown to my office. My office! Phew how posh! I was also introduced to the first computer I had ever touched. I was given a few days coaching from the previous lady and then I was left to it. The computer was an old Commodore 64 with a tractor feed printer. I was the only accounts person and receptionist. The boss used to handle the general ledger and all that advanced accounting stuff.

I soon grew to know the sales patter for windows and doors as opposed to that of the store.

A lady came in, followed by her stooped little man. She wanted purple window frames.

"I'm sorry madam, we don't make purple ones although we do a navy window frame. It will look quite smart and you will be the first one in that street to have navy blue windows and they will look lovely with your lovely white lace curtains".

"Well I did have my heart set on purple with purple drapes but I suppose it will do".

I would be trying to keep a straight face as I had caught a glimpse of the husband's relieved look and him wiping his brow with relief.

As the business grew so the computers and programs needed to change and I had to teach myself as we went through all those changes.

It wasn't too long before another girl was put on to reception as I was getting very busy. I had to learn the payroll as I have been doing them by hand to computer, and then needed to set up the program so that the pay would go straight into the men's accounts.

As the payroll got bigger, before this computerized system, I was required to take my car to work. I needed it to pick up the payroll. Not because it was heavy but for security purposes. I would need to be shut in my office with no interruptions until I had allocated the money into each man's pay packet. It was then double checked by the General Manager.

I needed to be at work at eight a.m. each day as we dealt with tradies and they started at that time. This continued until I finally had to leave because of ill health.

The receptionist would come in at nine a.m. and I could then get on with my own work. I grew with the business and enjoyed the challenge of learning new computers and programs and the extra jobs.

I then became credit manager which was a real challenge for me as I was still very shy. I found it hard to phone people and ask them to pay their bills. Towards the end of my working life I was responsible for getting hundreds of thousands of dollars in so that I could transfer hundreds and thousands of dollars on a particular day. We needed to have that money on that exact day to be able to claim a discount. This would mean a great deal of money to the company.

The sales Manager and I set up the company credit policy and it was my difficult task to police it.

As the years went by, I was working fewer days. I would need to have a day off to collect my strength for the next day at work. Eventually the doctor said I would be eligible for disability pension. Many people said, "Oh it's very hard to get that. You won't get that".

When I went to be assessed by an independent doctor he said that you needed a certain number of points to obtain that pension and I had gained far in excess of the required number.

During this time we had moved house as the owner wanted to sell the one we were living in.

We found this nice house with a very nice landlord, who had agreed to keep the rent down a bit to get someone in he could rely on. We made quite a few changes both inside and in the garden with his permission.

One thing I delighted in was a room across the back, as the veranda had been glassed in and on a winter's day, the sun streamed in through those windows and it was lovely and warm. We put a table and chairs out there and I had my lunch there every day. Even in the summer, with the windows wide open, and not too much sun on the glass it was beautiful too.

I still miss that sun room and hope that one day I again will have such a room facing the right way to catch the winter sun.

WIDENING THE BACK
DOOR TO THE GARAGE

When we first moved into that house and Tony was married, I became involved in a direct marketing business.

This business was growing quickly with the help of very good friends. I drove to Portsea one day to help my group there, and do a few meetings.

The friends who had helped me were proud of me doing the meetings on my own.

This night, I had left Portsea quite late and by the time I was nearly home, I had the windows wide open and was singing loudly to myself to keep awake.

I pulled into our driveway at around midnight. I stopped in front of the garage and thought I would leave the car out. However, for some reason I must have changed my mind because the next thing I knew, the car was nose first into the apple tree behind the garage.

Evan came racing out, "Mum! Mum!"

It must have been a terrible shock for him as he was sleeping in the bungalow attached to the garage and would have been woken by a sound like a freight train coming through his room. It must have sounded like it anyway and then finding his mum slumped over the wheel of the car with its nose buried in the apple tree. What a shock for him!

He phoned his brother whose wife was a nurse and they came racing down. D was checking me out for injuries and I said,

"Look after Evan, he must have had a terrible shock".

I think we were all in shock then. All people could say is, "What happened? What did you do?"

I can only think that, having decided to put the car away after all, I was going to move it back so I could open the garage door. I must have put my foot on the accelerator instead of the brake and when I felt it move forward, slammed my foot down on the wrong pedal. I had ploughed through the closed front doors and through the back door which was not really designed to drive a car through, only to be stopped by the apple tree! If it had not been there, I would have been through the neighbour's fence and into their garage.

The insurance company could not work it out when we tried to explain it and they rubber stamped it to be inspected. The car and everything had to stay put until they came.

I think, on finally arriving home, I had lost my concentration and determination and just gone to sleep.

This finally put an end to my travelling long distances and with my health becoming worse, my business slowly faded. It was a real shame as that was another challenge I was enjoying and really believed I could have built it to a higher level.

ONE MEDICAL ANSWER

After that accident, I struggled on, going to work when I was really too ill. The management presented me with a warning letter. For the sake of the company I knew that I must address my health problems. Going to the doctor he said I had a virus. I asked how long a virus could go on for and he said if it was 'Ross River' or one of those it could continue and keep reoccurring.

I then showed the doctor the letter from my boss and he then made a lot of other tests. He found that I had an overactive thyroid and said that they would knock it out with radioactive iodine. It was not an enlarged thyroid gland like a goitre but was overactive. An operation was out of the question as it was too close to my voice box.

It took two doses to knock it out and from then for the rest of my life, I must take tablets to keep it high enough to be safe.

After that little episode I did improve, but then became more and more tired.

House Sharing again

It was about this time that I came across a man who had married a one-time school friend. He had played with a band that came to Swift's Creek for dances and also helped Eric Moore with the pictures.

He had been divorced for many years and had just come out of a long relationship.

After going out for coffee at one time and then to a meal, it progressed to me cooking a meal for him sometimes. We remained good friends and one day he asked me to share the house with him to help with expenses.

This worked out OK for a while but with my health getting worse, I would spend every second day in bed in order to get fit enough to return to work. I was cooking all the meals, doing the housework and the shopping. I would go to work, then do the household shop and would become very irate when I had to make several trips to the car and back to bring the shopping in.

He would be there watching the television after having read the paper from front to back. I did not say anything to him as I just wanted a quiet time with no arguments.

He would sometimes get the huff and not speak to me for several days without explaining to me what the problem was. Maybe he considered that It was his house and I should be doing everything to make up for it. We did share all expenses. I also painted most of the rooms in the house and made a nice garden.

PLAYING GRANDMA

When I was notified of my pension eligibility, my daughter and her husband asked if I would like to come and live in Traralgon. They would purchase a unit, and, in exchange for rent, I was to look after her small children. I was thrilled in one way. Until then I had been envious of the other mothers-in-law who could be grandma to the other grandchildren because they didn't work. I had only been able to spend a short time with any of them because I had to work. The worst thing about this was leaving my youngest son and his lovely little family in Bairnsdale.

However this is life.

The new life went well and I formed a wonderful bond with those two boys, as I was seeing them almost every day. Sharon had another baby sitter who had them one day per week to give me a break.

This continued until kindergarten for the eldest, when I would take him and pick him up. The same with the other one until they each went to school. They would then come to me every night after school.

Sharon's business grew and grew and I'm so pleased I was able to help then.

I joined a choir after Mum's death.

Luckily, when it was time for me to come into a nursing home, they were at high school and able to look after themselves. They each have busy lives with them both having paper runs and sport on other nights. There is also homework to contend with now. I miss seeing them every day.

Nursing Home

I had been having home care for quite some time, but the time was coming when I needed much more help. I had been approved for extra help and further help was coming soon.

I was using a walking frame to get around outside but had some falls in the house. With my legs having no strength, I was unable to get myself onto my feet. One day I fell in the lounge room and had to shuffle on my bottom until I reached a chair to pull myself up. I had an alarm which I wore around my neck but I guess I regarded it as only for emergencies.

Another day I fell in my bedroom. Fortunately I was unhurt as I had just glided down as the bed rolled away from me. I had to stay there until my grandson came home from school as I couldn't get to anything which would be strong enough without tipping over. It must have been a shock for him to find Grandma on the floor in her bedroom. He dashed out to our neighbour and together they got me up. That boy is very sensitive and he probably told his mum how upset he was.

My rheumatoid arthritis was becoming worse and the osteo in my back was making it almost impossible to walk far or sit in anything other than my lounge chair with cushions piled up. I also had fibromyalgia which made my arms and thighs very painful. Another result of this disease is the chronic fatigue, which is like your batteries going flat and having no way to charge them. Sometimes I need to take tiny steps and it takes ages to get from A to B.

I then began to get unpleasant turns at night, It is very hard to describe but it seemed like I didn't have enough breath. I had this sinking feeling inside which caused me to kick my legs, walk around and shake my arms to try and get rid of it

I was roaring like a bull and stiffening up, arching my back. I had to keep trying to move or something to relieve that feeling. I rang the alarm and told the lady I was having a fit. She said if I was having a fit I wouldn't know about it. She rang the ambulance and I asked them not to phone my daughter as she was not aware of the first bad turn. When they put me on oxygen in the ambulance, I felt a bit better. When we got to the hospital without the oxygen, that feeling came back. They said I had enough oxygen in my blood so didn't give me any more.

One of the paramedics said he thought it was like an overdose of thyroid medication. He looked up his book and said he thought that's what it was. After doing tests and X-rays etc. they sent me home.

Next time it happened I asked that they phone Sharon and she saw me having the attack. She said my body could not take too much of that. She was very upset. I have had a few minor attacks since but I've been able to see them through. The hospital doctor said it was a panic attack which I strongly disagreed with. Why would I wake up in the middle of the night with a panic attack. What would I be panicking about then? My doctor said I wasn't to be left alone at night. One night Evan came down all the way from Bairnsdale to spend the night with me, as there was no-one else available. We tried to get some sort of overnight nurse visits or to find some other way of enabling me to stay at home. We could find no other alternative but for me to go into a nursing home. We visited each of the facilities but the only one which had a respite bed available was Glenwood.

The only reason for my writing this is to try and explain why I needed to go into a nursing home at sixty nine years old. I am not looking for sympathy, just understanding.

After a few months, my preferred choice of facility had a room available and I transferred here.

I am settled in here and am able to take part in the facility's Resident Representatives Group and am the secretary.

The Staff are wonderful here and we are looked after very well.

The activities available to all residents are being upgraded and changed and they are really making an effort to have something to interest everyone.

I have not taken part in many of these activities except for classes for things I have had experience with, but I try to assist with the teaching.

The reason I have not taken part in the activities is because I have been writing and have just published my first book. When my book, 'Sanctuaries United' was accepted for publication, I was ecstatic and could barely believe it until I had my first copy in my hands. It has been a wonderful learning curve for me in that the experience has taught me a lot to take forward to this book.

I had actually begun this book and was quite a way towards finishing it when the other popped its head up and insisted it be written instead! I told it to wait its turn as I wanted to finish this book first. However it kept at me until I gave in and started writing it. It started as a short story and grew and grew until it became a book. A small one maybe, but still a book.

It was a most exciting time and my first signing here at O'Mara House was made possible because of the help of Diane who did all the posters and set up the whole thing. Thank you Diane.

I have been extremely busy dealing with the publishers of my first book and the marketing of it. In the middle of all this, I have been franticly trying to finish this book, 'Where Waters Meet'.

Did I tell you why this name for my book? Riley's Creek met Swift's Creek up above us almost to Cassillis and the Swift's Creek met the Tambo river right behind the township of Swift's Creek.

Until the next book, take care and share the love.

So with a signing in Traralgon tomorrow I'll leave you for now. Until next time, keep on reading and smiling, and I hope you enjoy this book as much as I have enjoyed writing it.